THE NOUVEAUX PAUVRES

A GUIDE TO DOWNWARD NOBILITY

THE NOUVEAUX PAUVRES

A GUIDE TO DOWNWARD NOBILITY

Nicholas Monson & Debra Scott

Quartet Books
London Melbourne New York

First published by Quartet Books Limited 1984
A member of the Namara Group
27/29 Goodge Street, London W1P 1FD

British Library Cataloguing in Publication Data

Monson, Nicholas
The nouveaux pauvres.
1. Upper classes—Great Britain 2. Great
Britain—Social life and customs—1945–
I. Title II. Scott, Debra
941.085'8'0880621 DT653.G7

ISBN 0-7043-3458-5

Typeset by MC Typeset, Chatham, Kent
Printed and bound in Great Britain by
Mackays of Chatham Ltd, Kent

Acknowledgements

The authors thank everyone who has helped them, in particular the following who have been so generous with their time and effort: Lady Serena Andrew; Lady Elizabeth Anson; Naim Attallah; Richard Barber; Andrew Barrow; John Brooke-Little; Lord Burghersh; Fred Carr; Susan Clarke; Ian Dunlop; Dominic French; Sarah Greenwood; Adam Helliker; Karen Humphries; Fiona Irwin; Anthony Jasay; Lord Kingsale; Allyson Longe; Charles Marsden; Margot Norman; Alastair Pirrie; Timothy Platel; Camilla Scott; Peter Townend; Hugo Vickers.

This book is dedicated to
the authors' maternal grandmothers,
Nicholette Devas and Gaye Campbell.

The Nouveaux Pauvres was first conceived by
Nicholas Monson and Debra Scott when the former
was the Editor of *The Magazine*.

List of Contents

THE NOUVEAUX PAUVRES

AN INTRODUCTION

Lord Kingsale, Lady Megan Edgecumbe, the Honourable Patrick Sinclair, the Countess of Mar, the Earl of Ypres and Lady Kenilworth are a sample of the British aristocracy. Guess how they spend their weekdays:

Do they hunt, shoot or fish? No. Do they fly off at whim to holiday in the sun? No. Do they lounge about beneath gilded portraits in stately homes? No. Do some perhaps recline in a fat-paid sinecure in the City? No.

They have been working respectively as a silage-pit builder, a council gardener, a busdriver, a British Telecom saleswoman, a hall porter and a dental hygienist. All are representative of a new British tribe – the Nouveaux Pauvres.

The Nouveaux Pauvres are the increasing numbers of the British upper classes, with middle-class, and lower, financial clout. Although by the national average, NPs cannot be considered poor (with some exceptions), by their own ancestral standards, they are a depressed minority.

For every gilded aristocrat chronicled in the gossip pages of the popular press, there is a less publicized peer or baronet living off the waning glory of his ancestral past. Some dwell in the crumbling wing of an Elizabethan manor, others have retreated to terraced houses in obscure London boroughs and others still are reduced to bedsits.

Nowadays a married man with two children and two fully furnished houses needs at *least* £80,000 a year net to live a comfortable patrician existence. The members of the nobility and gentry who can claim the resources 'to do all the right things' are becoming ever fewer.

Born and bred as an upholder of gentility, the NP is cut off from the life to which he feels rightfully heir by punitive assaults on his fast-dwindling capital. 'Money these days is in totally the wrong hands,' NPs moan, and what was once a taboo subject for conversation or even inner speculation occupies an ungentlemanly proportion of his thoughts and efforts.

But avarice is not enough to guarantee the recouping of his former station. NPs are not bred to soil their noble hands with money. Their gentlemanly reflexes, an undoubted asset in the club smoking-room and on the pheasant drive are, however, a deadweight in commerce.

There is only one class superior to the Nouveaux Pauvres: the Ancien Régime. Though both are equal on social ground, the few dwindling members of the Ancien Régime have managed the prodigious feat of holding on to their money. Unlike NPs they have triumphed over the latterday menaces of Capital Transfer Tax, costly divorce and debilitating inflation. The crucial difference between the two groups is that NPs concern themselves with trying to make money (or more usually thinking about trying to make money) while members of the Ancien Régime concern themselves with trying to keep it.

The NP may still own land, stocks in the family business (long since taken over) and a house filled with valuable antiques, but because of intractable trusts and complex laws of entailment, he is almost always legally denied the right to sell any or part of his inheritance for a reasonably profitable sum. His trust fund or annual allowance covers (not in all cases) the minimal costs of his life, yet he is still unable to afford to live in the style to which his progenitors were accustomed. Even *with* capital he has 'an ongoing cash-flow crisis'.

The NP man was prepared at home and school for a life of languid gentility: loafing at his London club or hunting and shooting relentlessly on his estate. The NP woman was prepared to be an aristocratic passenger, at best her noble husband's domestic impresario. Instead they find themselves somewhere on the wrong side of both upper-class inertia and working-class drudgery. Flawlessly programmed for leisure, he has to work and she to scrub.

Yet even with this new phenomenon called a salary, he still cannot afford what he considers the basic goods of noble life and what his social underlings consider luxuries. Ineffably perplexed that his well-honed accent, outstanding sports career at Harrow and network of family friends have allowed him to end up making his own tea in a Wandsworth basement, he has faced up to his sorry predicament with a fortitude worthy of his breeding. The once and (he hopes) future man of fortune is reduced in the present state of the Empire's affairs to a life of vicarious pleasures, nostalgic reveries of bygone splendour and ingenuous delusions of imminent retribution.

The gentry and the aristocracy have always had their financial ups and downs; yet never in the nation's history has the tide of affairs conspired to make it quite so down for the upper crust.

Yet when NPs do face up to the 'wrongful parting' of their 'rightful wealth', it is more in the spirit of strategical withdrawal than defeated resignation. Most NPs remain irrepressibly optimistic believing 'something will turn up' whether in the form of a love-struck nouveau riche, oil being discovered beneath some family bogland or the benevolent will of a geriatric aunt.

In order to acquire some of the things his tutored life was meant to provide, he has had to develop the distasteful art of compromise. Though he is well aware of the financial depths to which he has tumbled, for the sake of appearances the NP devises selected bluffs. His priorities are stringent: he would brave a blizzard before stooping to wear nylon pyjamas; he would forgo salmon before selling his signet ring; he would more willingly repay his gambling than tailoring debts; a boiled egg at his club would be preferable to a four-course meal at a Berni Inn.

There are many grades of NP, depending upon the heights from which he or she has originated to the depths to which they have fallen. The forthcoming chapters explore the genteel and occasionally brutish world in which the NP is called upon to make heroic sacrifices. More than a Who's Who of Who Hasn't, it illustrates how high NPs aspire and just how low the upper classes will allow themselves to fall from their noble ideals.

HERITAGE

The Nouveau Pauvre was born with a silver spoon in his mouth. This gave him great comfort for he was told he could do many things with a silver spoon that those without one could not. Yet wherever he went and whatever he did jealous people would mutter indignantly: 'Oi! Look at that toffee-nosed git, bawn wiv a silver spoon in his marf! 'Oo's 'e think 'e is, then?'

Then one day he noticed the spoon was getting a little tarnished. And so he took it out for a good polish. He was in for a rude shock. The NP discovered that all along the spoon had only been silver-plated!

So the panic-stricken NP rushed out into the market-place to sell off its minuscule coating of silver. Unfortunately some brash and distasteful Texan was selling silver short and had driven the price to an artificial low.

He then went to see what he could get for it in the jobmarket. But was told they wanted only sharp knives or pointed forks . . . and made out of stainless steel.

The NP searched and he searched. But could find no one who wanted his silver-plated spoon. And to this day the NP has still not found a buyer. And as he wanders aimlessly about, his spoon protruding from his mouth, he still hears the familiar refrain: 'Blimey! Look at 'im then. Stuck wiv a bleedin' silver-plated spoon in his marf! 'Oo's 'e think 'e is, then?'

The moral of this story is: There's not much demand for silver plate.

FAMILY PORTRAITS

The family portraits of countless generations of ancestors hang from every conceivable space throughout the ancestral house. The most distinguished hang in the dining-room. Their scowls, forever frozen by Van Dyke's and Kneller's brushes, glare intimidatingly down upon their descendants as the latter discuss the affairs of the nation while supping on fish fingers and scrambled eggs. Bedecked in gold-embroidered doublets and pearl-encrusted skirts, they seem of a time so affluent, so distant, so foreign that the NP family now dismiss them as more remote than E.T.

In the drawing-room hang the present family's portraits, daubed in inferior pastel (half the cost of oils), commissioned by Father in a rare moment of indulgence.

MOTHER As the indisputable *grande dame* of the community, she does not allow the damp patches on the drawing-room walls nor the peeling paint to irk her. Her chief topic of conversation is 'the extraordinary price' of the item she has most recently purchased. She drives a battered Peugeot estate car, and when behind its wheel stares with a withering condescension at the parvenu occupants of any passing Rolls.

FATHER Discovered economies late in life. He conscientiously collects rubber bands and string, muttering as he picks them out of wastepaper baskets 'Waste not, want not', yet he still buys his footwear at Lobbs. When he ascends to that great big parkland in the sky, most of his earthbound parkland moves off as well – to his creditors and the Inland Revenue.

FIRST SON He lives in Fulham and works as a badly paid auctioneer of Fine Art. Yet he still retains the haughty confidence of his forbears. This is because he is smugly aware that short of committing some scandalous sexual atrocity, the estate will pass to him alone. He has yet to learn about the mortgage arrears.

SISTER At twenty-eight she is still hunting Lord Right though she's now thinking of settling for Mr Almost-Acceptable . . . if he comes along. The fun of cooking directors' lunches in the City and sharing a 'jolly house' in Battersea with two secretaries and a china restorer is beginning to wear as thin as the leather on her Guccis.

THE YOUNGER SON There is no portrait of him as he was working his passage to Australia at the time the portraits were commissioned. There is, however, a slightly out-of-focus Instamatic photograph taken of him at a sheep station in Alice Springs. His mother has framed this and placed it on a table in the infrequently-used library.

FROM MANSION TO MAISONETTE

AN EVERYDAY STORY OF A YOUNG NP

Whatever his and his sister's premonition of the future, the typical NP child grows up with the full privileges of aristocratic life. It is all very splendid indeed (referred to as 'comfortable' by his parents). He roller skates through halls hung with Mortlake tapestries. That little piece of bric-a-brac he once carelessly knocked over was Quattrocento Venetian glass. Not only did his backyard serve as a receptacle for discarded cricket bats and rubber ducks, but it also incidentally contained fun things to play in and around like gazebos, Roman temples, drawbridges, moats and assorted Gothic follies. His most frightening memory is of the time he was lost for hours in the Thomas Hill maze.

Here at home 'young Master Randolph' first encounters the working class (in the form of his servants) and from a tender age develops the Common Touch – the polite yet firm way to deal with them. This facility will be handy in later life. Not that he'll employ any of the working class himself, but because he'll almost certainly find himself working alongside them. It is also at home where he forms his rarefied taste for Tintoretto skies, Grinling Gibbons carvings and vintage port – cravings that make it so difficult for NPs to assimilate happily into the philistine lower echelons.

One day, as he's riding to hounds without

ever having to leave the family estate, it occurs to Randolph that his days at home are numbered. His parents smooth this traumatic adjustment with helpful hints:

- They present him with a map of Australia for his birthday . . . and the following night, details of APEX fares to Sydney are lain casually on his bed.
- They bestow upon him a leather-tooled edition of Samuel Smiles' *Self Help* (which he later flogs at Bonhams).
- They lease his bedroom to an American tourist for the summer.

And soon they thrust him from the gilded nest into the cruel world. Clutching the address of a friendly godparent and a London *A–Z* Randolph enters the realm of NPdom. His first port of call is the family solicitor, also the chief trustee, who in 1966 wisely invested for him a small sum in an up-and-coming firm called Rayonworth. To the mild bewilderment of the solicitor, who blew the dust off the portfolio for the first time that morning, that small sum is even smaller – six times less, taking into account inflation. The solicitor curses himself for not keeping the money in one per cent fixed Empire Bonds. After scribbling calculations on the back of a writ, Randolph's trustee benignly awards him a weekly allowance of £21 and announces that he can look for a property to the value of £13,000.

Perusing the property pages in a give-away glossy magazine, Randolph quickly realizes that he can hardly afford an Earl's Court bedsit, never mind a comfortable flat off Sloane Square. So placing his capital on bank deposit, he seeks out old school chum 'Bunjy' Belborough. Fortunately for Bunjy, his trust had bought him an artisan's house in Parson's Green at a time when artisans (and NPs) could afford them, i.e. before rich media types decided Fulham was trendy. Bunjy's wine-merchant salary is so low that he needs to take in lodgers.

Randolph finds that £30 a week gets him not only a bed and roof but also dinner-party privileges, the use of the coin box on the stairway and a chance to pinch Bunjy's girl-friends. He can also take advantage of his landlord's subscriptions to *Tatler* and *Country Life*.

Borrowing a bespoke suit from Bunjy 'only one size too small', Randolph attends an interview at a top estate agency. Dropping the name of a grandee relation or two he is immediately propelled into the exciting world of flat-flogging. Soon his evenings are taken up swilling plonk and swapping shrewder-than-thou glances with fellow property 'dealers' in Draycotts and other Chelsea wine bars. Occasionally Randolph dashes off 'to close a deal' with such firm-jawed determination his colleagues think he must be selling a mansion to the Aga Khan, when in fact he's only showing a punter around a Pimlico basement.

Once a month he clambers out of his pin-stripes and into his tweeds. Journeying back to the parental pile he is transformed into a 'weekend squire'. In this transient feudal role 'Mister Randolph' oversees the dipping of a few sheep, reprimands some ramblers who unwittingly trespass on his father's sugar-beet field and fires off a box of cartridges winging the odd pigeon and rabbit – all before returning to his box of a bedroom in London.

One day while reading a gossip column and sniggering over the indiscretions and misfortunes of other nobs, Randolph is jolted by an item about his own parents, who, he reads, have sold off their last Van Dyke to finance some Colefax and Fowler curtains. It dawns on Randolph that with the present generation squandering 'his' inheritance, he'd better 'make a killing in the Big Smoke' if he wants to live 'decently'.

That night at a bring-a-bottle party in Battersea he bumps into a suave commodity dealer who auspiciously confides to him that he has just 'coined it' in Magnesium futures. So the following morning Randolph appears at Barracuda Commodities Inc. with his savings. Having expected a major windfall, Randolph is dismayed when his broker rings him the following week to explain that his discretionary account has *only* risen by fifteen per cent. Soon after, as he is ogling the details of a Tuscan villa, he receives another phone call: 'I'm afraid Titanium is tracking back, old boy. Still I've a hunch about mangoes! Listen, your account needs squaring. Send us round another five G.'

Months later, during that time of year his great aunt still calls 'the Season', the bankrupt Randolph is sent a free ticket to a charity dance by Lady Dragonwell so that he can meet her daughter. During the hoolie at Grosvenor House Randolph ignores the rich but ugly Miss Dragonwell and bestows his attentions instead upon the charming and blonde Annabel who boasts of 'plans to start my own decorating business'. A year later they marry.

Pooling their resources, they acquire a 'charming maisonette in Wandsworth' in a street 'with great character'. And characters in that street welcome the couple by promptly burgling them. Settling down to a routine of nightly television suppers and weekly dinner parties, Randolph continues to peddle property while Annabel occasionally matches curtain fabric for working friends in Stockwell and Clapham. Constantly inquiring about the 'health' of their rich and sickly aunts, Randolph and his wife live hopefully ever after.

■

THE NP CODE

All NPs are gentlemen and a lot of gentlemen are NPs of varying levels of deprivation. Some might belittle the term gentleman as archaic but for the NP it is all he has left to distinguish himself from everyone else.

Where once he possessed thousands of acres, he now retains little more than impeccable manners. But in today's brutish environment, the NP finds decorous conduct as hard to keep up as his ancestral seat. In the face of unpayable bills, impertinent VAT men and irreversible dry rot, the gentlemanly code has had to be redefined for the NP age.

Certainly the technical definition of a gentleman as 'one who lives off unearned income' no longer applies. It is true that many of the more old-fashioned NPs maintain their livelihood is 'earned' where the only work they do is to brandish a letter knife, slit open an envelope and withdraw a cheque (even when it happens to be a Social Security one). But today, most NPs, where and if they can, work for a living (if inhabiting a Chelsea basement can be considered living).

These are some of the NP adjustments to the gentlemanly code of conduct:

Manners

They maketh man and mollify the bank manager

Trust

A word is a bond but a signature is a cashable security

Honour

Honour those who honour their cheques

ACCENT

Who wants to learn how to speak with a plum? One or two misguided nouveaux riches perhaps, but there are no real job possibilities here for the NP. Outside the club and the drawing-room, an upper-class accent can be a liability.

Studies made in the field of speech show that the nasal twang of the upper classes excites more hostility than any other British accent. Up to the Second World War, the power base was instinctively perceived to be in the upper- and middle-class camp so the upper- and middle-class accent was consciously or unconsciously emulated. In the late fifties the power base was seen to shift perceptibly downmarket and so by the mid-sixties the upper-class accent was fast diminishing and vocal consensus was found in flat regional tones. The upper-class accent became a minority accent – an accent with a stigma.

According to recent research at Bristol University, those who spoke with an upper-class accent (an 'Oxford' one) were perceived to be more intelligent than those with other accents (good for the NP); but, by the same token, were thought to be more unpleasant (bad). According to the research the accent had connotations of snobbishness, pomposity and occasional nastiness. No doubt this was partly aggravated by the media. Children's comics from the mid-sixties onwards delighted in the theme of a snotty upper-class brat getting his come-uppance from ordinary street kids. And in advertising, which is in the business of harnessing prejudice, the upper-class stereotype chinless wonder has often been (and still is) used as a fall guy to help a product get sympathy.

An extreme expression of this bigotry was channelled against a fourteen-year-old schoolgirl called Lorraine Walker whom the press dubbed 'Little Miss Posh'. For the pains of her sub-Julie Andrews vowels a concerted campaign of vilification had her driven out of her school and then neighbourhood. Though extreme, the case is not unusual (see Education).

Alas for the upper- and middle-class accent, it's not even that welcome in its own environment. On radio the Duchess of Devonshire expressed shame about her accent, referring to it as 'silly'. But according to the research, this sort of rejection of one's own accent is not aberrant but commonplace. After comparisons abroad they discovered that the prejudices attached to any 'minority' accent are not dismissed but *believed* by those who speak with it. In Canada the 'minority' accent is the French Canadian. Those who speak with an English Canadian accent (the dominant one) say the French Canadian accent is a reflection of stupidity – the stronger the accent, the more stupid they are. Absurd, but this prejudice is no less willingly aired by French Canadians who taunt their own kind with allegations of asininity. So too with the British upper classes. Watch them wince with embarrassment when hearing an upper-class accent more plummy than their own.

How does the upper-class accent affect the NP? It can stop him getting jobs and when he gets them it can make him (or her) a scapegoat. Minority accents are soft targets (see Office Politics).

But if his upper-class accent is a handicap in certain jobs, it still keeps the NP dominant in the nation's drawing-rooms. He knows so long as he still looks the part, one word from his mouth will paint a thousand ancestral pictures. Dreaming listeners will conjure up the image of the NP as squire overseeing expansive pastures from the saddle of a favourite mare, or a vision of him browsing through a first edition of *Pilgrim's Progress* while reclining on a Linnel chaise longue beneath the imperious gaze of a Titian portrait.

How graceless it would be for the NP to disclose the depressing truth that the closest he came to scanning expansive acres was in the property pages of *Country Life*. Or that the last time he was gazed at by a figure in a Titian painting was on a visit to the National Gallery. Or that his copy of *Pilgrim's Progress* is long owed back to the borough library.

But vocabulary, just as much as accent,

gives the NP away: the noble wine salesman showing friends round his Wandsworth semi-detached refers to his 'chimney-piece'; when the elderly NP scrutinizes the fit of his hired dinner jacket, he is surveying himself in a 'looking glass'; when a dowager tunes into the World Service, she's switched on the 'wireless'. The NP feels that if he's reduced to living in lodgings meant to house a grocer, then at least the walls can reverberate with words that spill from the lips of a duke.

Like his vocabulary, the NP's accent is more than an instrument of illusion. It is a banner of his assumptions and values. To have downward elocution lessons, like the Earl of Dudley's niece, the actress Rachel Ward, might make for a more comfortable assimilation into modern Britain, but it would also be symbolic of defeat, a betrayal of beliefs he still holds dear. By not being true to his accent, the NP ceases to be true to himself.

PRIMOGENITURE

Until death duties and capital transfer tax, most noble families managed to keep their fortune intact from generation to generation. This was achieved through primogeniture, the heartless expedient of cutting out daughters and younger sons from a slice of the clan lucre and passing the hog of the estate to the eldest-born male.

In the past the privilege of primogeniture carried with it the moral duty to look after one's brothers and sisters. It was not done for the heir to gorge, drink and debauch off the fat of his land while poor relations eked out a threadbare existence elsewhere. They too would sit at his table, gorge and drink but the heir would also see to it that a fruitful sinecure or rich spouse came the way of his kith and kin. Sons and daughters of rich tradesmen were then only too eager to 'better' themselves by marrying an aristocrat albeit an impecunious one. Alternatively there was always a rotten borough that needed representing or some stretch of the Empire that needed governing. But such sinecures and spouses are now sparse on the ground and certainly not within the powers of today's feudal barons to fix for their brothers and sisters.

The best most family chiefs can do is to instal their close relations in trust-owned properties and perhaps, if they can afford it, give them a small income. Till recently richer aristocrats like the Duke of Norfolk would even give cousins a supplementary income but the days of distributing largesse so expansively are over. Ulster King of Arms, John Brooke-Little says there might have been some poor aristocrats in the past but their relations always had enough money to look after them. He gives a striking example: 'The Duke of Norfolk's cousin, the Earl of Effingham, is presently reduced to residing in a bedsit in the Cromwell Road [the approach route for the M4]. In the past his present fate would have been unthinkable.'

Primogeniture is often attacked as being crude and undiscriminating as it can mean that a profligate and/or unsuitable eldest son inherits while a worthy younger one is passed by. The example that is often cited for unsuitability is the pony-tailed heir to the Marquis of Bath – pornographic muralist and campaigner for Wessex Home Rule, Viscount Weymouth. 'Whacky' Weymouth might well enter the history books as a colourful and amusing eccentric but common opinion is that his neglected surviving brother, Lord Christopher Thynne, would be a more respectable heir to Longleat, the magnificent stately home.

Like many aristocrats Lady Elizabeth Anson believes that a pernicious effect of primogeniture is to upset, sometimes even poison family relationships from as early as the cradle. Some among the upper classes go so far as to comment that even mothers and fathers can resent a blameless eldest son.

Columnist Auberon Waugh is another fierce critic of primogeniture. He points not only to the resentments but the guilts generated by this 'cruel and unnatural system' which he claims has 'historically divided the rich from the middle classes in a way which few other advanced countries have experienced'.

NPs debate the subject constantly. But the argument as to whether an estate should be carved up or passed down intact is entirely academic for most NPs as their families no longer own estates for this choice to be exercised.

Viscount Weymouth: the most appropriate heir to Longleat? *PHOTO: ALAN DAVIDSON*

THE FALL OF THE ARISTOCRAT AND THE RISE OF THE NP

(AS THE NP UNDERSTANDS IT)

A CALENDAR LISTING SIGNIFICANT EVENTS IN HIS HISTORICAL EVOLUTION

1789 The French Revolution
First tremors of egalitarianism break into full-scale rift

1832 The Great Reform Act
Out go Parliament's 'rotten seats' and the upper classes' control of local affairs

1880 The Farming Slump
Estates go bankrupt

1894 Death Duty Law Passed
The bleeding begins

1903 The Wyndham Act
The government acquires land in Ireland and hands it to tenants on easy terms

1914–18 First World War
The culling of great families and their estates

1925 Anthony Wedgwood Benn is Born
The first upper-class turncoat

1929 Stock Market Crashes
Many overnight NPs

1946 First Strong Labour Government
A new vanguard of Robin Hood and his Merry Men

1947 India's Independence
Where have all the outposts gone?

1964 National Service Abolished
Still possible to be a gentleman; less so an officer

1973 World Oil Crisis
Shares plummet

1975 Capital Transfer Tax Begins
Tax loopholes shrink

WHO'S WHO OF WHO HASN'T

KIND HEARTS AND PAWNED CORONETS

A HIERARCHICAL (LOWERARCHICAL?) BREAKDOWN OF NPs

In the past, as sometimes now, peerages were largely 'bought', either by sucking up to the monarch or later to a large political party. The recipient of this titular honour may have had to exhibit a modicum of merit in order to justify the title, but he also needed sufficient funds and acreage to support the extravagances of his position. The station of peerage bestowed, corresponded to the level of family wealth so that a duke would require more money to bankroll his exalted station than a lowly baron. The fifth Marquess of Lansdowne, Viceroy of India, was just one peer who sadly had to forgo his candidature for dukedom, for shame of having inadequate riches. So it is that those with lesser positions within the upper classes generally represent the highest number of NPs – legions of landless gentry and hordes of Stately Homeless Hons followed in decreasing numbers by batches of barons through to a few brace of dukes, a prince and princess.

PHOTO: RON BELL/PRESS ASSOCIATION COURT

RETRENCHING ROYALS

When, a few years ago, Prince Philip assured the nation that even the royal family were undergoing the discomfort of keeping up with inflation, no one could have guessed that matters would have deteriorated to the point where:

★★★★★ The Queen would feel the need to work to the heat of a one-bar electric fire . . . and serve only one glass of wine with each course at Balmoral dinners.

★★★★ Prince Charles would spend £46,354 *more* than his Duchy of Cornwall income (1982).

★★★ Princess Anne would moan that she couldn't afford a top-class horse for three-day eventing.

★★ Mark Phillips would have to have his equestrian activities sponsored by British Leyland.

★ The Queen Mother would be seen to wear the same blue coat and hat at nearly every royal occasion.

Poverty is perceived to be relative. A lifestyle that is lavish to a commoner is perhaps austere for those more at home with ermine than polyester. The Queen's personal possessions make her worth upwards of £50 million – some say as high as £250 million – but she has huge expenses. Not only does she have to spend carefully but now she has to cut back. Twenty servants had to go in 1982. And those that remain have to shiver along with their mistress, for even during the coldest periods, central heating is now switched on only intermittently.

To help the Queen and the other royals with their public expenses, the government gives the family an annual sum that in 1983 came to over £4.5 million. However some royals get a more substantial slice than others from the Civil List.

Poor Prince Michael of Kent receives nothing from it. So he has to generate an income, thought to be not far removed from £25,000 earned as a director of two companies. Such a modest stipend is especially problematic for Prince Michael as his strong-minded wife has difficulties mastering the bourgeois concept of 'economy'. However the couple do make savings through being social. Like many NPs, it is said of them they are more entertained than entertaining.

DISTRESSED DUKES

The misfortune of the Dukes of Leinster stems from a rash incident of post-obiting (a loan secured against future inheritance. See Last Resorts.) In 1922 the Duke's younger brother, Lord Edward Fitzgerald, had debts amounting to £60,000 (today's money: £810,000). Not wishing to be declared bankrupt, he made a deal with a canny businessman, Sir Harry Mallaby-Deeley. For paying off all his debts, Sir Harry was to receive the income from the ducal estates when Lord Edward eventually inherited, for the period lasting till he died. Alas for Lord Edward, just after he signed the agreement, his older brother died and he became the seventh Duke of Leinster. Had he not signed the deal with Sir Harry, he would have received in today's money a yearly income of £1.1 million. Under the agreement, though, he was to receive nothing.

The penniless Duke of Leinster lived on till 1976. 'There was virtually nothing left of the estate,' says his son Gerald, the present Duke. 'No, I am not bitter,' he adds, 'we all have our different furrows to plough in life.' The Duke's, till his recent retirement, was running an aviation company. His son and heir Maurice, the Marquess of Kildare, ploughs *his* furrow as a landscape gardener.

The present Duke of St Albans also inherited little. But on attaining the title from his eccentric cousin, Obby, he quickly went from being nouveau pauvre to retro riche by lending his name to some highly risky business ventures. Some of these companies folded up; others made a substantial profit. His estimated value is now £20 million.

The next dukedom predicted to slither into the ranks of NPdom is the dukedom of Somerset. The present Duchess, it is said, does *all* her own cooking.

MAKESHIFT MARQUESSES

The leading NP among marquesses is the Marquess of Tweedale. The Tweedale estate which used to run to tens of thousands of acres and, till twenty years ago a forty-bedroomed mansion in Scotland, now comprises a flat in London's North Kensington.

Throughout his twenties, the present Marquess, who took a degree at Oxford University, supported himself working as a labourer and bricklayer on building sites. The Marquess, whose father left him nothing, once had to go on Social Security. Now an insurance broker, he says he doesn't use his title much 'because it can be embarrassing being a marquess if you haven't any money'.

The Marquess of Bute's heir, the Earl of Dumfries, also works as a labourer and the plummy diction of the upper classes has been long forsaken for a hybrid Cockney glottal. But much as he tries to assimilate into the society of more ordinary folk, his anticipation of joining them financially is premature. The egalitarian Johnny, who at weekends is a sponsored racing car driver, stands to inherit an estate worth £80 million. Even after Capital Transfer Tax, he would be a long way from being an NP, though he lives like one now.

The Marquess of Anglesey is another peer who has had to give his ancestral home to the National Trust. His son, the Earl of Uxbridge, has a two-bedroomed flat in the trendy but downbeat London borough of Camden. A self-acclaimed 'hip capitalist', the Earl seems more influenced by the sixties than by his upper-class heritage. He runs a chain of poster shops. 'My family are far too enlightened to disapprove of me having gone into trade,' he says. The Earl is now trying to get his trustees to release some of his capital. 'It has a pathetic return,' he says. 'I am sure I could generate more money from it.'

ERODING EARLS

No aristocrat can be certain of his future as the story of the Earl of Breadalbane and Holland shows. His father was one of the richest men in Britain. He was the reputed owner of 365,000 acres in Scotland and he was waited upon by a large staff of servants in the magnificent Taymouth Castle where Queen Victoria spent her honeymoon. He died in 1959 and was succeeded by the present Earl, his only child, who had spent ten years in hospital after receiving a shrapnel wound in France while serving as an officer in the Black Watch.

Twenty years later a Sunday newspaper tracked down the tenth Earl to a bedsitting room in Finchley, North London. His living conditions were described as 'shabby and cramped'. The Old Etonian disabled war hero was existing on a weekly pension of £24 and a family trust allowance of £12.50. Apart from this latter sum, it appeared the ninth Earl had left his heir nothing. The beneficiary of the will, the dowager Countess, had instructed her solicitors to tell her son who, at one time to make ends meet, was reduced to playing a pipe in pubs, that a visit from him would be unwelcome.

What heinous crime had the Earl committed to be treated thus? None that anyone knows of. The Earl, who is too proud to claim Social Security, thinks that perhaps his family was disappointed in him. He is, it seems, simply an extreme victim of the perverse hostility that so often marks the relationship between the British upper classes and their offspring.

The Earl, whose trousers are held up with string, remarked that he rarely attends the House of Lords because his clothes are too shabby. 'I don't regret being an earl,' he says. 'I just wish I could afford to live like one.'

The grandson of the celebrated First World War general, the Earl of Ypres, is a confirmed NP. Rather than being depressed about his financial plight he has adopted a Monty Pythonesque sense of humour about his predicament. While employed as a porter in a Chelsea mansion block he would reply when asked whether the building was Peer Court, 'Yes, this is the peer you're speaking to.'

VALUELESS VISCOUNTS

Viscount Molesworth is the most established of NP viscounts. But he feels he is more ancien than nouveau pauvre, his ancestors having lost most of the family money in the earlier part of the century. Living in a basement flat in the socially unprestigious borough of London's N6, the retired Viscount worked most of his life doing clerical work. 'I most enjoy myself when I'm with the Georgian Society,' he says, 'looking at beautiful works of art in someone's ancestral home.'

Viscount Craigavon is another NP. Friends claim his tragedy is that he was born into the wrong class. 'Janric was the finest footballer that Eton ever had,' says a close friend. 'If he had come from working-class stock, he would have undoubtedly been a celebrated professional footballer of Georgie Best calibre and he would have earned a fortune.' As it is, the accountant-trained Craigavon earns little more than his attendance money from the House of Lords. He drives an old Austin 1100 and lives in a small flat in London's Earl's Court.

Viscount Chilston is another peer recently forced to part with his ancestral home. He inherited the beautiful Georgian mansion, 225 acres of lake-studded parkland, his title and a large tax demand in 1982. 'It's a gorgeous house that's been in the family for 160 years and I'm extremely sad to have sold it but its upkeep is beyond my purse,' says Viscount Chilston, a film producer who makes documentaries for the Central Office of Information.

BEGGARLY BARONS

The thirtieth Lord Kingsale is the Premier Baron of Ireland. His other family distinction is that his ancestors can lay claim to being the original NPs. His grandfather, he says, used to boast the Kingsales were poor before anyone else was rich, and with some historical justification: 'Do not bother old Lord Kingsale for he has no money,' it was written in the Court Rolls during Cromwell's reign.

Lord Kingsale, who lives in a Somerset cottage and works as the local silage pit builder, has a theory that the Nine Bards of Ireland are responsible for his family misfortune: 'Some distant ancestor made off with St Patrick's bones and they cursed him, vowing that the Kingsales would survive but always in poverty.

'The financial rot began when our family supported Henry VII and his stupid wars. Since then we've had opportunities to recoup the family coffers but have usually failed. My great-grandfather went out to Assam in India and succeeded in being the only man there not to make money out of tea,' he says.

Even when his family has had money Lord Kingsale says they never hang on to it. 'My father inherited half a million pounds and invested it in some company that distilled oils from bones. He left debts of £30,000.' Nor were his earlier ancestors any less profligate. One swapped Killbritain Castle for a rare white stoat.

Among his past jobs Lord Kingsale has worked as a Bingo caller in Stourbridge, Birmingham, a lorry driver in the West Country, an officer in the Irish Guards, a safari keeper on the Duke of Bedford's estate at Woburn and an Egyptian peasant in the film *Cleopatra* starring Elizabeth Taylor.

Britain's grandest silage-pit builder: Lord Kingsale. *PHOTO: ADAM HELLIKER*

Lord Kingsale blames his education for his inability to assimilate easily into the modern world: 'My education equipped me for an upper-class life of leisure, not working for a living. I wish I had been educated like my nephews who went to comprehensive school and have learnt about metalwork and carpentry. I've only learnt about such things in my early forties. I've recently learnt about plumbing and I do it occasionally for the local pub in return for free meals. It's this sort of practical education that most aristocrats will have to have in the future. Few will survive on their capital and they will all have to work like everyone else and quite right too. The country's class structure is anachronistic.'

As a hereditary peer taking the Labour whip, Lord Kilbracken works towards the end of the system altogether. 'The only worth of the title nowadays is that it enables one to sit, speak and vote in the House of Lords,' he says. It is a duty he takes seriously. 'What's the point of receiving imperative commands from the Queen to attend debates without taking advantage?' he asks.

Certainly Lord Kilbracken would not have much to lose materially if the manifesto of the Labour Party is carried out. Unable to afford to repair the ground floor of his Irish country seat, Killegar, which was destroyed by a fire in the early seventies, he lives entirely on its first floor. He never inherited any capital to maintain the house and the 400-acre estate. 'It never occurred to my father to put money in trust for future generations. Anyway I told him that I could take care of myself which pleased him immensely,' says Lord Kilbracken, who throughout his life earned his living as an author and journalist. To provide for his second son (thirty-eight years younger than the first) Lord Kilbracken fears he may have to sell his estate before he dies. His heir then will have no revenue but his own to support his half-burnt ancestral seat.

Lord Kenilworth, who runs a contract gardening business, inherited only some sticks of furniture along with that title. His glamorous wife supplements the family income by working as a dental hygienist. With the detectable pride of the self-made man Lord Kenilworth declares: 'My home [a terraced house in Fulham] is the product of pure hard labour.'

BATTERED BARONETS

Nouveau pauvre baronets abound throughout the globe. Leaf through Debrett's Baronetage and observe the numerous family trees, rife with noble intermarriage, culminating with the incumbent baronet living in some lowly borough, obscure provincial town or remote stretch of the once British Empire: Sir John Cockburn in Wandsworth; Sir Saville Burdett in Solihull (his house is poignantly called 'The Farthings'); Sir Basil Fraser in Deal; and Sir Edward Sharp in Swaziland.

The most spectacular crash of any baronet in recent times is Sir William Pigott-Brown who was twice Britain's amateur champion jockey. He lost his 2,000-acre Berkshire estate (worth £5 million), a stud farm and a string of racehorses when his property company, the aptly named 'London Bridge' followed the fate in the children's nursery rhyme, falling down with debts of over £7½ million.

But there are some busted baronets battling back up. Sir Marmaduke Blennerhasset's family have had no money since 1895 when his great-grandfather went bankrupt. His grandfather worked in the colonial service and his father as an engineer. In the thirties depression the sixth baronet was made redundant. 'He survived,' says Sir Marmaduke 'because he was amusing and was consequently invited to endless house-parties.'

During the Second World War, his father, who had enlisted in the navy, was killed at sea the day Marmaduke was born. After a then unusual co-educational boarding-school upbringing, Sir Marmaduke attended McGill University in Canada, where he trained as a geologist. There in Canada he had some 'graveyard luck': a distant cousin died, who, having no other relations, left Sir Marmaduke her Irish estate. It was lucky for Sir Marmaduke she even knew he was a relation. Their common ancestor lived over 400 years ago.

Sir Marmaduke managed to get enough money selling the crumbling west-coast estate to buy a house in Chelsea. The London-based Sir Marmaduke settled into work (like so many titled NPs) as a front man for a foreign-owned investment firm in the City. 'I was given a small salary and high commission,' he says. 'But it was an unsatisfactory career. I found I was always working to pay off an accumulating overdraft, instead of building a capital nest egg.'

One of the first things he did as a businessman was change his Christian name. He took up his second name Adrian instead. 'I soon discovered no one in Britain takes you seriously with a name like Marmaduke, certainly not when coupled with a surname like Blennerhasset,' he says. Because of the sixties property boom, Sir 'Adrian' estimates that he is now worth £200,000. Selling computer security systems from his present Chiswick home, he thinks that life would have been much grimmer had he not received the unexpected inheritance. But he is also grateful for another asset: 'By not going to a proper British public school,' he says, 'I am free from the restrained attitudes of my contemporaries who did. Judging from what I have seen, had I too been steeped in the traditional upper-class ethos, I doubt I would have survived.'

THE LANDLESS GENTRY

The biggest number of NPs belong to the gentry, the cousins from the collateral branches of the British aristocracy. Few inherit much at all and so, like the rest of the nation, have to make do, the best they can, on their own abilities. Of those we spoke to, Alastair Pirrie, an old Harrovian, was one of the most interesting, typifying so much of the prototype persona of the NP.

He has a distinguished provenance. On his mother's side his grandfather was the last clan chief of Carmichael. On his father's side he is a second cousin of Comte de Labrosse. Until two years ago when he inherited a house

Old Harrovian butler Alastair Pirrie serving one of his occasional masters – pop star Trevor Rankin. *PHOTO: TRACY CHAMOUN*

overlooking Brompton Cemetery on the fringes of Chelsea he lived on a trust allowance of £20 a week. He now runs his house as an art gallery selling the work of young painters. Because of low overheads he can afford to charge low prices. The buyers, he says, are a lot of the old English upper classes who can no longer afford to buy from West End galleries. But sometimes he doesn't make enough money from this enterprise so he lets off three floors of his house to pop stars. At the time we visited him, he had leased most of the house to lead guitarist Trevor Rankin of the Yes pop group (it is calculated Trevor's next album will consolidate him as a millionaire). But even letting his house sometimes doesn't pay Alastair Pirrie enough and so he often returns to the work that he had been doing for five years previously – working as a butler and footman.

'I must say that when I left school I had expectations of slipping into a comfortable and easy job. The reality was very different. But rather than face the prospect of some grisly job in the City for which I was temperamentally unsuited, I tried to get a job in the arts.

'Unfortunately it is very competitive and one has either to be brilliant on one's subject or have excellent contacts or more usually both. So I decided instead to use my skills of social decorum and work in service.

'My first job was serving as a footman at the dinners hosted by the *Sunday Times* in the Gray's Inn Road. Harold Evans and Lord Goodman were two of the faces that I recognized and there were lots of other people who behaved as if they were frightfully important – though whether they were I never knew. What was interesting was that so few of them knew how to treat a servant. They were either aloof or rude and abrupt. This actually didn't surprise me as most of them hadn't been brought up properly and so they didn't know any better. I just found it funny and ironical. And when I spoke they were completely thrown by my upper-class accent.'

Alastair Pirrie's accent got him into trouble at his next job which was serving as a footman at Castle Ashby for Lord Compton before he became the Marquess of Northampton.

'At the time I was hired, Lord Compton was abroad on honeymoon. I had been there about two weeks when the telephone rang. The voice asked to speak to the butler. So I asked who was speaking and he replied "Lord Compton," so I said "Certainly, my lord," and then handed over the phone.

'According to the butler, Lord Compton was highly agitated. "I never knew we had any guests staying," he said. "We don't, my lord," said the butler. "Then who the hell was I just speaking to?" "My lord, that was your new footman." "My new footman!" spluttered Lord Compton. "He sounds as if he owns the place, not works for it!" Things didn't work out after that and a fortnight later I left.'

His next job was in the Scottish highlands working as footman for the Marquess of Linlithgow. Pirrie had to bring him his early-morning tea. He describes the Marquess as 'a charming man, considerate to his staff in every way'. Then one day he received an invitation to a deb dance that had been forwarded by his mother.

'It was on an estate nearby. I decided I wanted to go but nobody, including the Marquess, knew about my background and I thought the footman requesting permission to go to a grand highland ball might rock the household's social equilibrium. Luck had it though that that night I had the evening off anyway so I quietly slipped off in my black tie to the dance. Everyone was most amused when they found out that I was Linlithgow's footman.'

King Rechad of Tunisia, with fiancée.
PHOTO: ALAN DAVIDSON, ALPHA

FRAYING FOREIGNERS

Alas for the Queen's cousins, those exiled foreign royals: they are now nearly all NPs. Few of those who managed to make the psychological adjustment from King to commoner have adapted comfortably to the consequent material deprivations.

The late King Zog of Albania found paper currency so mystifying that faced with a large bill he would pay with a diamond picked from a bucket where he kept the crown jewels.

The exiled King Farouk of Egypt gambled away an annual income of £2 million. His sister, Princess Fathia, who went to America, kept herself by scrubbing floors and married a commoner who later shot her dead in a seedy Los Angeles boarding house.

Finding London property prices too exorbitant, the Sultan of Zanzibar moved his court in exile to Southsea near Portsmouth, where he lives on an unroyal income of about £10,000 a year.

King Rechad of Tunisia toils for London stockbroking firm Hoare Govett. He says his income is about one per cent of the revenues he would have had if he had remained on the throne. Deposed at the age of five, the karate-black-belt King thinks he has little chance of returning to power, though it is said that the rulers of Tunisia are perturbed by his ability and eagerness to break up breeze blocks with his bare fist.

Prince Michael of Romania is unemployed and looking for a job. An ex-salesman for a Wall Street brokerage firm, his compensation from the Romanian government was, he claims, under £50,000. 'It's hard for a king to find a job,' he once said. 'Do you know of anything that might interest me?'

An ex-captain of the British tank division,

Crown Prince Alexander of Yugoslavia now works as a middle-management insurance executive in Chicago. His wife Princess Dona Maria is daughter of Prince Dom Pedro, claimant to the throne of Brazil. Supplementing the family income as an interior decorator, Princess Dona Maria says she is glad that her husband was left virtually nothing from his father, whose late career as a businessman was a failure. 'I wouldn't have married you if you had two million dollars,' she tells him. 'You would have been spoiled. Who wants to marry a rich prince?' Prince Alexander, who says he has to make it entirely on his own, lives in a condominium and owns little else but a half share in a lakeside country cottage.

Claimant to the Russian throne, Grand Duke Wladimir has little money of his own either. 'The story of there being Romanoff treasure in the Bank of England is phony,' he says. Indeed the only known wealth the Romanoffs took with them, he says, was the Empress's jewels which were sold for a mere £10,000 to the Queen Mother. The miffed Romanoffs say they often see them being worn today by Our Majesty Queen Elizabeth. Fortunately for Wladimir, he married Grand Duchess Leonida, who inherited from her first husband a not insubstantial part of the Woolworth chain.

In England most foreign princes are NPs. Prince Nicholas of Prussia has moved from Chelsea to a terraced house in the brave new borough of Battersea. The genial Prince Aly Khan of Hyderabad whose great-uncle, the Nizam, was the richest man in the world, lost most of his fortune speculating on gold and is reduced to renting a single room in a flat off Sloane Square. Prince Galitzine runs a small PR company in Belgravia. And Prince Peter Sapieha is a sales director of publishing company Bodley Head and shares rented accommodation in Montagu Square W1. Like most foreign princes living in Britain, he says he has no private money at all – 'just a few family baubles'.

■

MONEY

THE PRICE OF DOING ALL THE RIGHT THINGS

'A gentleman can jog along on
£40,000 a year.'
(Today's money: £900,000 p.a.)

▪

THE THIRD MARQUESS OF HERTFORD (1777–1842)

Pay to
NP

THE GENTLEMAN'S ACCOUNTS

The assumption of the yearly accounts of the prototype gentleman is that he supports a non-working wife and two children until they are twenty-one. He owns two handsome but not extravagantly decorated houses with antique furniture, paintings and silver. One is a six-roomed house in London SW3 and the other a Georgian manor in North Wiltshire with fourteen rooms, a three-acre garden and a paddock. The capital value of the houses and their contents is £500,000. The gentleman has no mortgage on either house; their only cost is the upkeep. In his other outgoings, the gentleman is almost austere by the standards of some of his noble neighbours. He has no yacht, no racehorses and no hunting expenses, though he does belong to a shooting syndicate. He doesn't drive a Rolls-Royce, keep a mistress, gamble or maintain any costly hobby or vice. His wife does not demand a lavish wardrobe, nor does she expect or ever receive expensive gifts of jewellery. The children are privately educated, though neither is unduly indulged. A married couple living in as butler and cook look after the country house. The butler doubles up as the gardener and the cook helps out with the housekeeping. To manage the children and assist her generally the wife takes on an au pair. The family take two holidays a year and every November the gentleman takes his wife to Venice for a long romantic weekend. Both husband and wife like to dress well and eat well. Within their own terms they are not extravagant. They are just 'doing the right thing'. What does it cost? £80,000 a year.

To receive this money net the gentleman has to make £185,000 gross. There are a few commercial nabobs in the City who earn this amount, but most of the upper classes hardly earn a quarter of such a sum. Of course many have private incomes, though only the richest have ones large enough to subsidize the difference. But up until the last fifty years or so, only an exceptional minority of the upper classes did *not* have substantial private means. In real terms, half had as much as the £80,000 required for a noble existence today. Some had much, much more. In 1881 a social commentator, Grenville Murray, advised upper-class mothers launching their daugh-

THE SUITOR'S PRIVATE INCOME (WITH MURRAY'S VERDICT)

£2,000 a year (£54,000 in today's money)
'Gilded misery'

£5,000 a year (£135,000 in today's money)
'Comparative pauperism'

£10,000 a year (£270,000 in today's money)
'Would do for want of anything better'

ters on the acceptability, or otherwise, of the private incomes of their daughters' suitors. It is interesting to see that he regards the bottom line for financial comfort as over three times today's minimum amount. All the incomes are in addition to owning property.

Grenville Murray in fact warns mothers and daughters to forgo any of the measly incomes above and advises them to go straight for a coronet (a peer) and £50,000 a year, which in

YEARLY OUTGOINC

THE LONDON HOUSE

Rates	£2,000
Electricity	£350
Gas (central heating and hot water)	£750
Telephone (including country one)	£950
Home insurance	£700
Cleaning woman (three days a week)	£1,200
Renovation, redecoration, upkeep on roof etc.	£800
Plumbing and electrical maintenance	£200
Au Pair/cook/help	£3,000
Household goods	£700
	£10,650

THE COUNTRY HOUSE

Rates	£1,000
Electricity	£400
Oil-fired central heating	£3,500
Two domestic staff living in (including employer's NIC)	£8,500
Renovation, redecoration, upkeep on roof etc.	£1,200
Plumbing and electrical maintenance	£200
Home insurance	£950
Household goods	£600
	£16,350

HIS WIFE

Hairdresser	£800
Shoes	£300
Lingerie	£200
Make-up and scent	£250
A Renault 5 (including tax, running costs, insurance, service, parking, depreciation etc.) on hire purchase	£2,500
Three designer outfits for weddings christenings, Ascot etc.	£1,500
Two evening dresses	£1,500
Three hats	£240
Jerseys, silk shirts, country clothes	£550
Spending money (lunches with friends, presents for godchildren, nephews, nieces. etc.)	£1,500
	£9,340

TOTAL COSTS FOR 'DOIN

today's money would be £1.35 million. Today's NPs would be glad to have only one per cent of such a private income.

Nor is Murray the only chronicler of the nineteenth century to have reservations about the above table of private incomes. In 1832 Nimrod's *Life of a Sportsman* revealed that a gentleman was almost pitied for possessing such a 'comparatively limited' income of £10,000 a year (today: £220,000).

OR TODAY'S PATRICIAN

HIMSELF

Two suits (Huntsman in Savile Row)	*£2,000*
Shirts and ties (New and Lingwood)	*£500*
Shoes (from Church's and one pair from Lobbs)	*£600*
Casual clothes, underwear	*£500*
Restaurants	*£3,000*
Membership of Annabels and Whites	*£500*
Nightclubs and gentleman's club, expenses other than membership	*£2,000*
Membership of shooting syndicate	*£2,000*
A BMW (including tax, running costs insurance, parking, depreciation etc.) on hire purchase	*£4,500*
Haircuts	*£60*
Spending money	*£1,000*
	£16,660

FAMILY

Fortnight's skiing holiday (Easter in a three-star hotel)	*£4,000*
Three weeks' summer holiday in South of France	*£2,700*
Long weekend in Venice (just husband and wife)	*£1,000*
Food (to include domestic staff)	*£4,000*
Wines and spirits	*£3,000*
Son's education till twenty-one (averaged)	*£3,000*
Daughter's education till twenty-one (averaged)	*£2,500*
Upkeep, clothing and pocket money for children till twenty-one	*£2,500*
Recreational expenses of children	*£1,000*
Laundry	*£800*
Dry cleaning	*£600*
BUPA	*£600*
Doctors and dentists	*£600*
Newspapers, magazines and comics	*£250*
Books, records	*£450*
	£27,000

HE RIGHT THING': *£80,000*

TILL DEATH DUTIES DO US PART

From his nursery days onwards, the NP was bred never to discuss money. He would more easily raise the subject of fornication at a vicar's tea party than debate the merits of alternative City investments at the dinner table. While his family remained rich, this snobbish quirk never really mattered but on becoming poorer, the NP found that lack of discussion about money meant that he and his kind were often profoundly ignorant about this crucial phenomenon. Of late, however, money has become an acceptable subject for NPs and at their drinks parties there is much earnest waffle about fluctuations in gilts, equities and futures. Yet to the tutored financial ear, the average NP's grasp of how money works parallels a bus conductor's knowledge of heraldry.

NPs forever live beyond their means because they cannot adjust to not being wealthy. They are not 'grasping' in any vulgar sense. It is just that they were brought up to expect certain things, which, irritatingly, the absence of this obliging matter, money, denies them.

An NP would concur that it is not money that is the root of all evil, but the lack of it.

CREDIT CARDS – AMERICAN DISTRESS The NP claims to abhor the invention of money's plastic cousin, though usually in his time he has had credit cards in abundance: 'They're a good way of prolonging the pain,' he'll say. Also lesser untitled NPs are delighted the way that certain credit-card companies will happily print the pretentious misnomer 'Esquire' after their name, which serves to intimidate shop assistants as well as to bolster the NP's legitimately shallow confidence. But the NP finds those innocuous flimsy rectangles can lead to a painful time with gentlemen whose methods of credit control don't classify them as such. The credit-card company that NPs particularly fear is American Express. However, it is the accumulated interest that persuades the NP to jettison this costly means of spending: 'You'd get better terms from Shylock,' is the current NP refrain as he rips one or all of them up. But this prejudice does not apply to bank cards: 'They're essential for cashing cheques, old boy!'

CASH – TO THE TENNER BORN NPs have had to learn to deal in this highly suspicious currency. The days were when his name was the only promissory note he need sully himself with. When paper money was first issued, an eccentric member of the upper class, Squire Mytton, exhibited his disdain for it by eating it in sandwiches. Other nobility who held it in higher regard had their butlers iron it with their newspapers.

CHEQUEBOOK PATERNALISM The NP prefers using cheques to hard cash – cheques being the nearest modern-day equivalent to promissory notes. Chequebooks are not, however, always easy to retain. Occasionally it is necessary to humour those who honour them. But some NPs find it is not within their social repertoire to humble themselves even before the most agitated of bank managers. The grand stepsister of an earl, Fiona Irwin, regrets to this day the unfortunate exchange that took place with her bank manager, which, because of her unyielding

aristocratic principles, turned out to be their last. She had just been on a customary spending spree, when he called her in for an urgent discussion:
HE (*visibly distressed*): 'Madam, do you realize the state of your account?'
SHE (*brushing aside the proffered statement*): 'I have never known the state of my account and I have no intention of starting now!'
HE: 'Very well, madam, you'd better hand me your chequebook.'
All things considered, Miss Irwin does now consider this an inconvenience.

ACCOUNTS The crucial word in the NP's financial repertoire is 'account'. He holds many with St James's tradesmen. In his glorious past, accounts were something the estate manager looked after, so it is no surprise he has such a confusing time sorting his out. His favourite excuse to tradesmen anxious to have his account settled is that his 'bloody trustees' are late paying his quarterly disbursement. For honour's sake, when he is in funds, he'd rather pay off outstanding gambling debts than his tailor's bill.

BANKS The NP's biggest account is with his bank. 'Overdraft' is a word he has had to stoop to acknowledge. Particularly down and out NPs are humiliatingly refused them as they are told they have no 'surety'. Should he not have family connections with a director or partner of 'the small three' (Coutts, Williams & Glyn and Hoares) he may bank instead with one of 'the big four' (the High Street banks). If he has an account with the latter, the NP who needs a long line of credit will pick a branch near the family estate, or, if that's been sold, near to his richest relation, because he reasons: 1) the bank will be reluctant to bounce cheques for fear of repercussions with the plutocratic branch of the family; 2) provincial managers are more gullible, and ready to swallow yarns of 'big deals in the Square Mile' from those with eminent family names. This ploy rarely works for long, though, before the NP is sent irritating reminders that the NP is banking with them and not the other way round. For these NPs, their rancid relationship with the bank is matched only by that with their building society.

DEBTS Debts are what the NP accumulates in abundance though he would rather refer to money owed as *credit* – 'helps with the cash flow, what?'

In the past the upper classes were usually magnanimous to those in debt to them. They would rather forgo repayment than be embarrassed actually having to *ask* for it. But in today's tough world such tender sensibilities have had to go the way of the Russian monarchy. A stately home tour operator owed tens of thousands of pounds to clients who included Countess Spencer and Lord Brocket. She finally met her Waterloo at Inverary Castle, home of the Duke of Argyll. Just as she had finished a decorous drawing-room tea party with the Duke and ten Americans, His Grace blocked her exit with his foot and said: 'Now could you please give me the sum agreed. If you don't, I'll throw you in the dungeons.'

BAILIFFS A bailiff was somebody the NP's family once employed for the tiresome chore of collecting rent from the estate tenants. Now it is somebody the NP dreads every time the doorbell rings.

The NP knows of no prescribed etiquette for dealing with these ill-bred henchmen of the law intent upon robbing him of the Augustus John sketch or Chippendale mirror. Some NP debtors pretend to be the butler and with stiff, unblinking countenance, inform the inquiring bailiffs His Lordship has recently left on a two-month motoring holiday on the continent. This ruse, though effective in the short term, is no deterrent, however, for the determined debt-collector.

When baronet's son Dai Llewelyn lost a court case and lacked the wherewithal to stump up a five-figure sum, persistent bailiffs, no doubt incited by their quarry's fame, lurked in piranha-like shoals outside his Harley Street front door. His wife, Vanessa, niece of the Duke of Norfolk, displayed admirable resourcefulness when coping with this threat to her family's possessions.

'I worked out a way of smuggling the silver out of the house,' she says. 'Each time I'd go out with the baby, I'd hide some cutlery or a candlestick beneath the pram's mattress. It must have been slightly uncomfortable for the baby but after a dozen or so excursions to relatives' houses, our Georgian silver was completely safe.'

THE TRUST The trust is the threadbare financial mattress between the NP and the frightening spectre of destitution. It may not keep him in the style to which he should like to feel accustomed but he is thankful all the same for the showers of lucre that help pay off all those boring domestic bills like rates, electricity, telephone and the wine merchant.

The problem for the NP is that the trust is not the secure ever-flowing well of funds he feels it should be. His income can fluctuate wildly depending on the wisdom of the trustee's investments (see Do You Trust the Trustees?) The NP often experiences acute trepidation anticipating what the postman will deliver. Chances are the NP has taken out a second mortgage, lost £300 at backgammon and acquired, in a heady moment, a GTI Golf on hire purchase . . . all on the strength of an optimistically high figure on the trust cheque.

Many NPs, however, have only a small trust that splutters out a small three-figure sum once a year. The trust is continued because the legal cost of breaking it exceeds its capital value. But the NP fallen on hard times can find this meagre supplement more of a hindrance than a help. Many an NP who has applied for legal aid or Social Security has been greeted with hoots of derision when admitting he has a trust. 'Trust' for most state bureaucrats implies a large cache of undisclosed lolly. Shrill protestations from desperate NPs are usually received with conspicuous scepticism by officials from Social Security.

CRI DE PAUVRE It is sometimes difficult to tell the difference between a genuinely rich member of the upper classes and an NP because nearly all upper classes today 'play poor'. Playing poor or 'cri de pauvre' is a fashionable game of inverted financial snobbery where each contestant attempts to outdo the other with protestations of how hard-up they are. Some go so far in this one-downmanship that they not only imply they are skint but dress it as well. The Duke of Devonshire has become an envied byword for his threadbare jackets and disintegrating collars. His Grace is hardly destitute, but his wardrobe has propelled tramps with upper-class accents into the height of fashion.

Cri de pauvre evolved from the old upper-class attitude to money – that it should be there but never talked about. Cri de pauvre

has adjusted the rules: it is still vulgar to boast of 'having' money but it is now a social accomplishment to whine about the lack of it. The upper classes started playing cri de pauvre in the mid-sixties for differing reasons. They felt it might

— Ward off the taxman
— Dampen indignant socialism
— Generate some sympathy from the working classes
— Distinguish them from the vulgar nouveaux riches

Cri de pauvre quickly caught on because a growing number of the upper classes were genuinely becoming poorer and it enabled them to do so without embarrassment. It also became popular with a lot of the old rich because cri de pauvre is an excuse for meanness and being miserly could help them hang on to what they had.

True NPs are, however, put out by the cri de pauvre moans of the wealthy. When the Duke of Westminster, whose approximate value is £2,000 million, complains he can afford only a *second-hand* helicopter, NPs are not moved to offer heartfelt sympathy. Nor was an NP family overwhelmed with pity when their dinner guest, the Earl of Lichfield, moaned of the trauma of having to sell his St James's town house. If only they had one to sell, they despondently reflected.

It is when they themselves are the victims of the 'economy drives' of their ultra-rich cousins that NPs become truly enraged. At dinner with some millionaire relations, an NP guest was lectured on the 'iniquitous price' of Colefax and Fowler silk fabric. 'They had spent thousands of pounds on new curtains and they served the worst plonk they thought they could get away with,' spluttered the indignant NP. 'I think it is disgusting pampering yourself while being mean with your guests!'

But this manifestation of cri de pauvre is not unusual. Dining with her shop-assistant daughter at the Berkeley Hotel, a grand lady from the northern shires spent the evening moaning about her lack of money. 'I'm so poor now darling,' she said 'we'll have to do without wine and drink water instead.' The following morning she flew to Paris to buy her spring wardrobe.

Ardent practitioners of cri de pauvre convince even themselves they really are poor. Small acts of self-deprivation imbue them with boundless self-righteousness. The middle-aged woman especially prides herself walking half a mile to save 10p on a tin of silver polish. En route, she might bump into a friend with whom she huddles to cries of 'Isn't it awful? Have you seen what they are charging for steak today?' or 'Can you imagine! My son living in a bedsit in Wandsworth!' They then briskly stride off and have an identical exchange when they meet up three weeks later in the stewards' enclosure of the local point-to-point.

PARENTAL MEANNESS Historically no son or daughter of noble loins could live a threadbare existence without incurring shame on their family name. But times have changed. Today it is not considered remotely incongruous when the Honourable Camilla Bauble-Stash is reduced to sharing a basement bedroom in Clapham, waitressing in the evening and buying her wardrobe from jumble sales while her plutocratic mama and papa holiday in Bali. Parental meanness is now an accepted social trait of the upper-class rich.

After their children's education is finished, noble parents find their heirs presumptuous when they request money to set themselves up. Surely those *exorbitant* school fees were paid precisely to educate them to earn it themselves? Haven't *they* 'done their bit' over the last twenty-one years?

So, all too often, Master Quentin and Miss Lavinia, the castle gates clanking shut behind them, are despatched into the world with just enough for a train fare to London. Do Lord and Lady Bauble-Stash fret with troublesome pangs of guilt over this miserly policy they have adopted with their children? On the contrary, this cavalier treatment of their brood prompts self-congratulation. It means they have not succumbed, like some vulgar nouveau riche, to *spoiling* the children. After all, a bit of deprivation is good for their *character*. They'd only *waste* the money if they had it. Quentin and Lavinia must make their *own* way in the world says His Lordship self-righteously, tucking into some estate-shot pheasant.

Throughout this discursive justification, it is conveniently forgotten that the last time anyone in his family 'made it' was in 1769 when the father of the first Viscount swindled the Stock Exchange, the proceeds of which his descendants had been living off ever since.

Should Quentin and Lavinia ever be so ungracious as to comment on the disparity of lifestyle between themselves and their mama and papa, Lord and Lady Bauble-Stash will simply point to hordes of NP neighbours who could hardly afford to help their children for a £50 driving offence let alone set them up in a London flat. 'Andrew and Priscilla Hasbeen only get £15 a month from their father, so why can't you survive on the same?' they ask. When Quentin and Lavinia point out that Sir Reginald Hasbeen is, unlike them, having to live off his naval pension, Lord and Lady Bauble-Stash retreat into 'cri de pauvre'. Identifying aristocrats richer than themselves, they firmly declare: 'We're not the Howard de Waldens!' (worth: £50 million), or 'We're not the Vesteys!' (£200 million) or (the favourite) 'We're not the Grosvenors!' (£2,000 million). It is an argument Quentin and Lavinia can never win.

But this financial meanness is not such a shock for Quentin and Lavinia; it is merely an extension of the emotional meanness that both were brought up on. Dogs and cats, they discovered early in life, hold a higher place in most noble families' affections than children. Parents were happy, they learnt, to acknowledge the polished surface of their offspring. But the unseemly aspects of emotional development were dealt with by Nanny, boarding schools and other convenient institutions. The aristocracy will never flinch from the duty they owe their children, but nowhere in the upper-class ethos does it dictate they have to love them.

So the vision of their children is selective. And the Lord and Lady Bauble-Stashes of Britain certainly do not elect either to understand or sympathize with the distasteful problems of their heirs being nouveaux pauvres.

DO YOU TRUST THE TRUSTEES?

'I am convinced that if any one section of the community can be held responsible for the devastating rape of the heritage, it is not the politician, nor the taxman, but surely the fuddy-duddy old family adviser.'

▪

CHARLES CLIVE-PONSONBY-FANE Esq.

When the NP is not badgering his trustees to advance him a little more capital he can often be heard at dinner parties bragging about how he is going to 'bust the trust!' This might be a terrific conversation-stopper but it is something the NP seldom gathers the necessary nerve to attempt. Though he suspects the trust isn't generating the sort of income *he* could get from it, he is wary of the aggravation and legal expense that would be incurred having the trust broken up.

The NP's trust was probably set up by his grandfather or father to make sure future generations were properly educated (i.e. sent to a good public school), and that the family acres were not squandered paying for gambling debts, an expensive mistress or some foolish commercial enterprise. Also until the Finance Act of 1982 discretionary trusts were an effective means of sidestepping the more pernicious taxes on capital.

But unmindful of the pains that his predecessor has undergone to protect him, the ungrateful NP concurs with other NPs that family trusts were vindictively devised as a legalized means of 'wrongfully withholding my rightful wealth'. He might go on to say that the trust was formed only because his predecessor couldn't bear the idea of his progeny having the lucre, once 'hogged' exclusively by him. He might even go on to speculate that the predecessor created the trust to achieve an *ersatz* immortality: that once he passed on, his power would none the less continue – a power to withhold by proxy.

Family trusts are a perpetual source of NP discontent, but it seems that few trust beneficiaries either do anything to monitor the trust's performance or set about breaking the trust if the performance is defective. And research indicates that the majority of family trusts' performances *are* defective.

The professional trustees who have the greatest influence on trusts are solicitors. Accountants and bankers can in certain cases have more say, but not usually. They can be divided into four categories:

1. The highly effective (rare)
2. The lazy or inexperienced (common)
3. The sharp (more common)
4. The dishonest (rare)

EFFECTIVE The highly effective trustees are so because they are monitored closely and the beneficiaries pay for expert advice. Such trustees and their advisers helped the family of Lord Vestey avoid generations of death duties and accumulate a fortune in excess of £100 million. It was also such trustees who helped the present Duke of Westminster come to be worth £2,000 million. The services of such trustees are expensive and they are thin on the ground.

LAZY The lazy or inexperienced trustees or, to put it kindly, the well-meaning but incompetent, are those who might make out payments in the wrong part of the year and so be hit by an unnecessarily large tax bill simply because they didn't bother to get advice from an accountant. Such trustees might also invest their clients' money in bad investments because either they didn't know any better or they've been too lazy to look around for better ones.

SHARP The sharp trustees often perform just as ineffectively with their clients' investments. The difference is that it serves their own interests. Example: as a solicitor the trustee might well be friendly with a building society who recommend their clients to him for conveyancing. So on a back-scratching basis, the trustee will in turn be tempted to place his client's money with that building society rather than another which offers a higher rate of return. Small London firms and provincial solicitors all have, to some extent, a symbiotic relationship with certain bank managers, estate agents, building societies and mortgage brokers. As such, a client's money is always vulnerable to this sort of practice.

The sharp trustee also looks for high commission. Technically commission should be declared but it can always be disguised or 'accidentally omitted' on the statement of accounts. The bigger the commission the more likely the investment that is chosen for the client irrespective of its return or security. Does one hear of many trustees investing in National Savings Certificates? Not many, if at all. There is no commission.

DISHONEST Then there are the dishonest trustees. These might well be solicitors in their mid-fifties and near to retirement. Wanting to salt away a nest egg, a cynical and amoral solicitor could well get up to the following ruse: he is asked to sell a trust property. Knowing that the beneficiaries either live elsewhere and have no idea or interest about property values (they might be retired or they could be children) he sells the property to a nominee company, perhaps in collusion with an estate agent, for sixty-five per cent of its value. Later it goes on the market for its full value. And the thirty-five per cent is taken as his personal profit.

ADVICE TO BENEFICIARIES So what does the NP do? He starts by examining the accounts and seeing how his money is handled. Too few make the effort. They take the attitude it is 'free money' and so consider it impertinent to inquire. NPs who have this attitude can blame only themselves for their trust not performing as it should.

The NP should, then, inquire about the terms of the trust. Trust law is strict and if trustees have failed in their duties or have in any way been negligent, they can be dismissed and in certain cases sued.

If the trust continues, however, the beneficiary can get a better deal from it in a number of different ways. Here are a few: if the trust is selling a property, there is no reason why an estate agency wouldn't take a smaller commission than the ordinary commercial one of two and a half per cent. For a sole agency most estate agencies will accept as little as one and a half. However the unprompted solicitor is not going to bother to ring round different estate agencies for a lower commission. Why should he make extra work for himself? It is not his money. Why should *he* care that the beneficiaries lose out on a possible £1,000 or so? So the trustee should be instructed to sell at a favourable rate of commission. If he still doesn't bother and he does not have a valid reason then he can be sued for the difference.

The trust might wish to invest in a certain building society. The beneficiary should then go and shop round for a more favourable rate of interest. If he finds one then the trust will have to have a highly plausible reason not to invest with it.

If the trust is going to buy a life-assurance scheme (an effective means of offsetting CTT) there is no reason why the beneficiary should not make himself the broker and receive the benefit of a large commission.

Ring up and ask the insurance company to appoint you as a broker. If they refuse, threaten to take the business elsewhere. Most should accept and you will be some few thousand pounds richer. (Some 'sharp' solicitors balk at this as they often get some sort of kickback from the brokers who arrange such schemes.)

Always find out what a trustee could be getting out of other investments too. The Inheritance Trust schemes that are presently being peddled carry *twice* the commission of any life-assurance scheme. Are they more effective? No. It seems the tax benefits of such schemes are dubious enough under present legislation, let alone future. So it is imperative to challenge trustees on choices of investment. Often it is not sharp practice that is responsible for a trust's bad performance, it is laziness and incompetence.

Old Etonian stockbroker Fred Carr, director of Capel Cure Myers, has many experiences of trustees. This was one of his most memorable: 'Two years ago I was approached by a reputable firm of solicitors to advise their clients on certain investments. *Seventeen* months later I received a telephone call saying the trustees' instructions had come through. I could proceed in acquiring shares in the firms I had originally recommended, provided my suggestions and subsequent confirmations were still valid!

'Events in the world and especially in the market-place move swiftly. Seventeen minutes can be critical for an investment – let alone seventeen months! The client had missed a good investment because of the sluggishness of his trustees. He paid a high price for having intermediaries between himself and an investment manager. In the time that had elapsed the shares had peaked, nearly doubling in price. They were no longer such a good investment.'

Like other financial experts, Fred Carr is not impressed by banks' performances as trustees – certainly not High Street banks: 'When a High Street bank is instructed to look after your investment portfolio, it simply sends it to the stockbroker allocated to the branch. If anything happens to your shares in between periodic reviews, you will not be advised. Thus your shares are almost certain to perform unsatisfactorily.'

If a bank does look after the trust then the beneficiary could do well to break it if possible – that is unless he thinks the trust is performing well. Banks charge three-quarters of one per cent minimum on the gross value of the trust every year. And when the trust is broken or is wound up then an extra two per cent is charged. But that is only the start. If they use their investment division then more is charged on top. And then the bulk of the work is passed on to a solicitor and accountant and the trust often has to pay for them as well. Frankly the beneficiaries might just as well go to them direct. But the solicitor or accountant won't advise them to do so. They don't want to upset the bank that is giving them so much business.

The NP simply has to remember the golden rule: Never trust the trustees.

▪

CLOTHES

FROM JERMYN STREET TO JUMBLE SALES

'The Duke of Devonshire is my pin-up man. He has lovely frayed cuffs and collars as if he had lent his new wardrobe to the gardener to wear in for six months. There's style for you'

▪

LADY RENDLESHAM
talking to *The Times*, 1983

NP MAN & HIS APPEARANCE

The imagined English gentleman in Huntsman and Lobb's. *PHOTO: JODY BOULTING*

The reality is the Duke of Devonshire. *PHOTO: CAMERA PRESS*

SITUATIONS IN WHICH THE NP MUST DRESS UP:

When sitting hours over one whisky at an hotel bar. (Staff are less apt to hurry him along.)

▪

When exchanging a suspiciously lived-in-looking article of clothing at a shop. (Such a favour is likely to be done only for an 'important' customer.)

▪

When at auction. (To discourage out-bidders.)

▪

When asking the bank for a loan of over £100,000.

The key to NP dress is SCRUFF. In the tolerant, anything-goes world of NPdom, he feels perfectly self-assured wearing the tattered garb that constitutes the bulk of his wardrobe. In fact, among themselves, NPs don't have a 'dress code' per se. They have an 'under-dress code'. To achieve this 'mean look' collars must be frayed, sweaters strewn with moth-holes, and ties must be generously spotted. The 'NP look' is not to be confused with the Viviene Westwood look where rich women spend fortunes for mock-tattered frocks. NP holes are not contrived: they are the genuine article. It is true 'slob appeal'.

There are times, however, when the NP deems it necessary to sheathe himself in the unfaded items in his wardrobe. It is a cruel fact that most non-NPs respond to the NP at face value. There exist people who, just because the NP looks like a tramp, will actually treat him as such. Whenever an NP expects to find himself in a vulnerable position, he compensates by appearing well turned out . . .

COUNTRY CLOTHES

The shabby appearance of country squires and ladies is often remarked upon by sartorially concerned foreigners, who point to the nobility's Worzel Gummidge-like wardrobe as an irrefutable sign of Britain's decline. However, it is not because the aristocracy cannot afford Yves St Laurent gumboots, but because they actually *prefer* to look scruffy in the country. Some, of course, assume the faded gentility look in town. When the fifteenth Duke of Norfolk was asked why he always dressed like a tramp he replied: 'It doesn't matter how I dress in the country because *everybody* knows who I am and it doesn't matter in London because *nobody* knows who I am.'

Today's most renowned aristocratic country 'tramp' is the present Duke of Devonshire, who is a byword for his frayed collars and cuffs. The Duke has been adopted as a sartorial patron saint for NPs. By promoting him as a chic peer, NPs can get away with looking like tramps themselves. Even such an authority on fashion as the London manager of Yves St Laurent, Lady Rendlesham, pronounced the dishevelled Duke to be a man of style. The crucial difference, however, between His Grace and his NP sartorial disciples is that the Duke could dress like a mannequin if he wished; NPs could never afford to.

So pervasive is the cult for dressing-down that a polo instructor called Michael Hanna gives his nouveaux riches clients pointers on how to transform their glaringly new country attire into worn and tattered garb.

HIS SUIT

The suit is one article of clothing on which NP man finds it hard to compromise. He would prefer one dilapidated but tailored suit to five off the peg. A hand-made suit, when the NP can afford one, has to last him a long time, which is why he always chooses the longer-wearing heavy fabric. The NP is fortunate that in Britain, at least, the state of one's suit rarely matters. Some gentlemen prefer suits like their pheasants: well-hung and nearly falling apart. Often some shambling squire from the shires is heard to say: 'I can't bear to wear a suit unless it's properly worn in.'

Gentlemen from the *ancien régime* invariably buy their suits from Savile Row. Savile Row must be one of the most valuable property sites in London and the prices the tailors charge reflect it. Huntsman is the most renowned but since so many of the upper classes are now NPs the British now account for only under 35% of their clients.

Nevertheless their premises at No. 11 reverberate to the sound of a hundred tailors chalking, cutting, measuring and stitching. The manager says it all happens under one roof 'so complete control can be maintained at all times'. Huntsman attribute the quality of their suits and clothes to the strength and construction of the stitching and they are probably right. The consumer magazine *Which* published a study comparing London suits. Their findings: Buy at Huntsman if you can possibly afford to. With few suits at under £900 not many NPs pay Huntsman regular visits. But some have them made up at the rate of at least one suit every five years.

This is not the foolish extravagance it might first appear. For the wise NP will have it copied in other fabrics and colours from cheaper backstreet tailors, who don't have Savile Row overheads. If the NP is very resourceful he might have it copied at Redmayne's in Cheshire, who advertise themselves in the classified advertisements of glossy magazines. Redmayne's will produce for the NP a suit for a third of the Savile Row price. But the NP can also find some surprisingly inexpensive tailors in London. Alternatively he might use his university or public-school tailor.

OFF THE PEG Some NPs, though, will buck their reflexes and stoop to buying suits off the peg. Even when he is not working, the NP's rationale for not going to his tailor is that 'the fittings take too long'.

The NP will usually buy his off-the-peg suits from either Moss Bros, Austin Reed, or Marks and Spencer. In the latter case he will excuse the acquisition by pointing out that they are the same suits sold at Harrods but cheaper. Very rarely will the NP venture out to flashy men's boutiques – the type now to be found in the King's Road, Oxford Street, Kensington Church Street and numerous towns in the provinces. It is not that the shoulders on the jacket go porridge-like and lumpy, nor that the lifespan of such suits, whose seams are fused with synthetic lining, is little more than a butterfly's. It's usually that the NP is appalled at the prospect of someone seeing, albeit accidentally, a vulgar and embarrassing name like 'Take Six' or 'Lord John' on the label inside his jacket.

When the NP does buy off the peg, he will spend up to £15 extra on making various adjustments, so that to the casual, untutored eye it might just appear the suit was 'bespoke'. He will change the invariably tacky plastic buttons for bone ones. He will cut a hole in the buttonhole (for an inexplicable reason nearly all off-the-peg suits have them sewn up), and he will add a fourth button to his jacket sleeves (non-tailored jackets have only two or three).

Of course the adjustments won't fool any of his upper-class brethren, but, recognizing the efforts he has gone to, they would be too polite to mention it.

SECOND HAND Though they affect to abhor 'off the peg', the ruling classes have no qualms now about buying their suits second-hand. During the last General Election, Edward Leigh, the Conservative MP for Gainsborough, campaigned in a suit he acquired for only £4. NPs concur that the best emporiums for recycled reach-me-downs are Hackett in the King's Road and Oxfam in Whitehall.

'I bought this charcoal Aquascutum suit at a village fête for £4,' says Conservative MP Edward Leigh. 'No, I do not feel a cheapskate. Mrs Thatcher believes in thrift and so do I.' *PHOTO: LOLO CHILD*

SHIRTS

NPs differ in their approaches to buying shirts. The *casual* NP, not out to impress anybody, thinks nothing of buying his at Marks and Spencer. He prefers the all-cotton ones in theory, though more often than not he settles for synthetic blends, which allow him more time on the cricket pitch and less at the ironing board. Though he enthuses over their relative cheapness, he also feels it his duty to grumble about their shortcomings. His biggest complaint is that the St Michael's brand has virtually non-existent tails.

On the other hand, the *traditional* NP fervently believes that a good shirt is as important as his suit. He feels that even if he is reduced to wearing off-the-peg suits with blushmaking labels like Gaylord or Hombré, a smart shirt can offset the sartorial damage (though not always rectify it). Jermyn Street is his shirt Mecca and his pilgrimages there always coincide with the sales. In Jermyn Street he gets the collar shape he desires, the arm length he needs and the double cuffs he likes to feel he can't live without. But he seldom opens an account at any of these shops for they usually require a minimum initial purchase of six shirts.

Enterprising NPs pride themselves on their resourcefulness in having pure silk shirts made for them in the Far East. A cousin or friend toiling for a merchant house like Jardine Matheson or Swires is sent the NP's measurements which are then relayed to some industrious oriental shirtmaker. NP man congratulates himself on his clever economy which, a month later, is erased by having to pay for an expensive dinner for the holidaying cousin/friend who arranged it all.

The traditional NP is a past master at extending the lifespan of a shirt way beyond its maker's expectations. As soon as it becomes frayed beyond the bounds of social decency, 'the little woman' i.e. the underpaid daily, is employed to 'turn' the collar and cuffs i.e. she reverses them so the fray becomes invisible. Lord Burghesh, sartorial man about town, remarks that 'not' turning collars and cuffs is a sign of 'inverted opulence'.

HIS SHOES

The NP's father had his shoes made for him at Lobb in St James. For the price of five pairs, today's NP could buy a decent second-hand car. These days Lobb's minimum price for a pair of shoes is circa £400. Who can afford them now? Not many British.

NP man patronizes the retail chain shop where he can get stylish though not always durable footwear. Ten years ago NP man could afford lounge-lizard Guccis – moccasin loafers with a dinky strip of brass chain over the instep. However the genuine article from Gucci is extremely expensive and, not unsensibly, High Street shoe shops like Clarks have cashed in with imitations. Genuine Guccis cost over £60. Imitations can cost under £20. These chic-looking loafers can withstand the longest drinks party and the deepest carpet pile. But when NP man treads them around the unresisting pavement they disintegrate in weeks.

One destitute deb's delight bought a pair at the beginning of 'the season' in mid-May. He returned them in early July and got a free pair from the concerned shop manager. In August he entered the shop with his soles flapping like disconnected flippers and got yet another. In September after another three and a half weeks of frenetic party-going he paid his monthly call to the shop whereupon the despairing manager gave him a complete refund. He then invested in a pair of slightly damaged shoes from Church's which have lasted him ever since.

Another NP device for Gucci loafers (and their imitations) is to put steel caps on the toes and heels. Though this directly contradicts the sartorial purpose of slinky drawing-room elegance an NP man will argue defensively that not only does this ploy make them last longer but it surprises 'the hell out of muggers' outside his home in Clapham.

HIS COAT

NP man knows he can always compensate for his lack of sartorial distinction by buying an ordinary wool coat and sticking on a velvet collar. If the rest of his attire is frayed or shabby, it gives him at least a louche aura of one who's once moved in moneyed circles.

Poorer NPs have made a fashion out of second-hand overcoats made during the Depression. Salesman recognize the particular nature of the NP: when selling him a tatty old coat they make astute comments like 'It was made for New York winters.' This adds a touch of foreign glamour.

HIS UNDERWEAR

Since NPs are notoriously mean with the central heating, thermal undies are *de rigueur*. Thermal undies come from Damart or from Marks and Spencer. As he is in the business of keeping up external appearances, NP man is nonchalant about what he wears underneath in warmer weather. This principle applies to other accessories. Ask an NP what's on the end of his watch chain and watch him blush when you discover it's a safety pin.

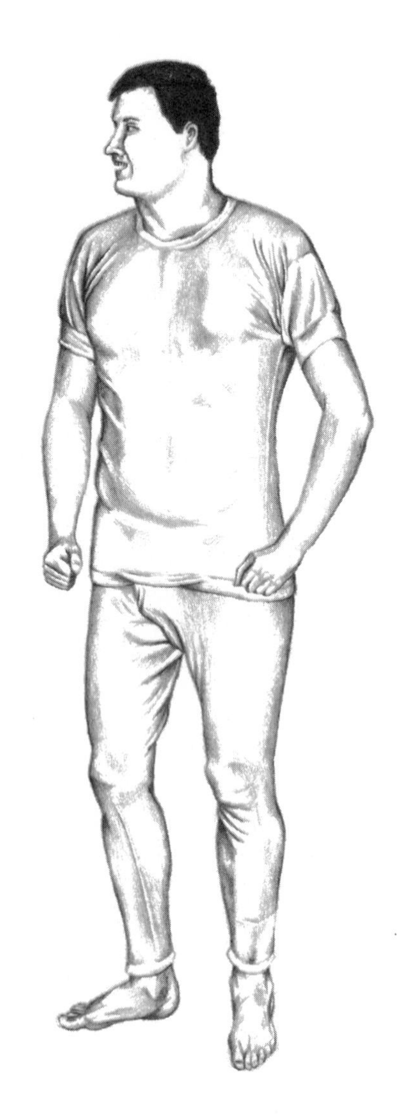

If, however, the NP's wife is Roman Catholic and seems bent on unaffordable procreation, he might well struggle daily into a fiercely tight pair of Y Fronts. This, coupled with volcanically hot baths, gives him, as he read in a problem page recently, almost certain sterility.

TIES

NPs know that it is bad form to go round waving one's Old Etonian or Old Harrovian credentials by wearing one's school tie – school ties being the province of minor public schools and those in 'trade'. However when feeling insecure and wishing to make a discreet point, NP man has not been unknown to wear his Old Etonian tie as a belt – a nonchalant but firm way to establish station (and it saves on leather).

WATCHES

Most NPs buy the cheapest Taiwanese watch they can find: 'All watches fall apart these days. If not, they get stolen, so why pay more than £25?' they argue. Other NPs look to the royal family for guidance. Luckily for them the royals are seldom flashy. It is only Prince Andrew who sports a Rolex. His older brother doesn't and it is him these NPs choose to emulate, so Rolexes are dismissed by NPs as being 'far too Finchley'. Their particular preference is for 'Flipper' watches which come with changeable plastic straps. NP woman particularly likes them as they come in enough colours to go with any of her outfits. 'They're so versatile,' she'll beam as she displays the thick cumbersome timepiece. Also: 'They're waterproof!' In the NP's eyes these attributes make them infinitely more attractive than any mere 22-carat gold watch with fancy Swiss workings.

AFTERSHAVE

The NP fears that anything more fragrant than hair lotion could mark him down as a pooftah. But he's been told that ladies go quite a wow for some of the foreign stuff, so at Duty Free he often stocks up on Monsieur Lanvin, Chanel for Gentlemen, and Eau Sauvage to save for 'that' evening. When he can't afford it he consoles himself that BO is unhomosexual and macho.

FLAIR IN MAINTENANCE

The most important duty in the NP's life is to hold on to what he's already got for as long as possible. Shoe polish and spare leather elbow-patches are key trouble-shooters in the NP's survival kit. Successful combat against cracking leather and fraying tweed is paramount when the funds to replace them are depleted.

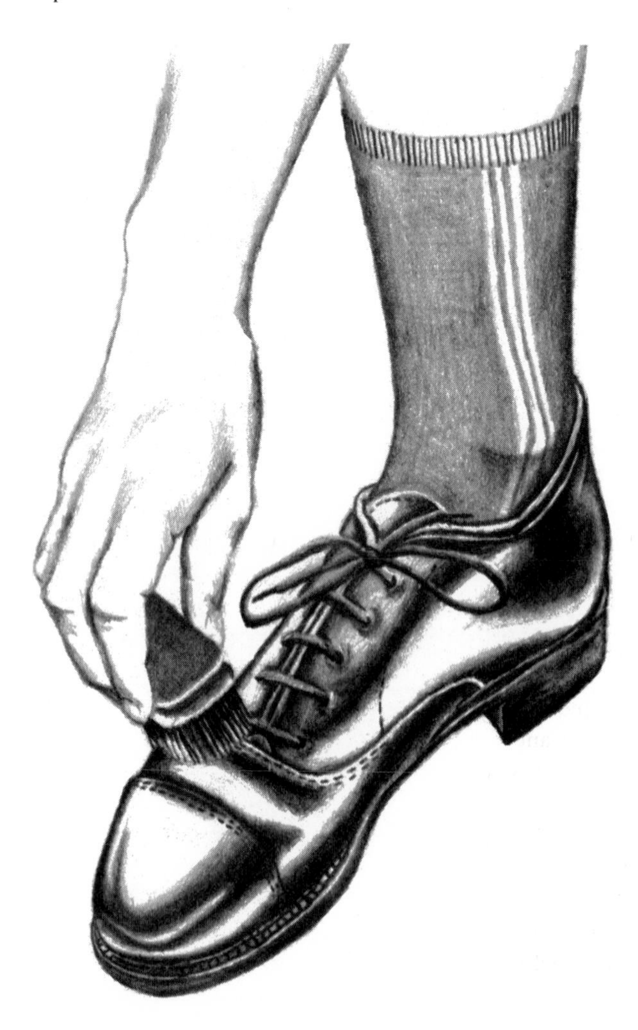

MAKING A CLEAN BREAST OF THINGS

The NP's greatest anxiety is taking his suits to be cleaned. The worst sin of a dry cleaner is to *over-clean*. This removes the essential oil from the wool and the life expectancy of the worsted starts to be diminished. The secret of a good cleaner is one who spot-cleans with a wet cloth. Should you overhear a customer closely questioning a cleaner over his spot-removing techniques, you can be sure it is an NP.

NPs still mourn the demise of Mr Foley near Regent's Park some years back; however, here are some London shops worthy of the former's discerning eye:

- ☞ *Lewis & Wayne:* Old-fashioned and comfortingly slow. Expensive but worth it. 13 Elystan Street SW3.
- ☞ *Scott's Hand Laundry Ltd:* They will collect from 'most' parts of London. 51 Market Place NW11.
- ☞ *Portmans:* They specialize in hand-finished clothes – even feathers. 17 London Street W1.
- ☞ *Mr Buttercup:* Customers never desert him. 49 Pimlico Road SW1.

NPs rarely go to Jeeves. They mistrust its archly snobbish name and they fear that its extravagant window displays reflect extravagant prices.

For some reason NPs enjoy swapping horror stories about dry-cleaning chains: 'I once took a ballgown to one,' says an NP woman (in fact, her *only* ballgown) 'and it came back a size smaller! *And* I was on a diet!' She lied.

VALET

NP man still retains a valet – not the sort personified by P.G. Wodehouse's Jeeves, rather the sort made out of wood. It stands deferentially in the corner of his bedroom, a suit jacket draped over it, allowing the air to blow out the smoke from last night's foray to Annabels.

SHOE POLISH & REPAIR

Though he may no longer require much silver polish, shoe polish is a must. An NP's dignity is measured by the clarity of his reflection in his shoes. Also it makes the shoes last longer. One NP admits: 'My life is very much ruled by shoe polish. It's in the car, everywhere.'

When most people's shoes start to disintegrate, they go into the dustbin. Not the NP's. Manufacturers hoping for a high turnover from their shoddy imitation Guccis would be appalled at how the NP makes them last so long, with surgery undertaken at the local shoe-repair shop (usually located in a dry cleaners or laundromat). Here the NP is confronted with making some quick decisions: should he or shouldn't he give in to his parsimonious side and get a rubber (horrors!) sole. But he usually doesn't; he knows it will make his feet smell.

NP WOMAN'S APPEARANCE

NP woman has cultivated the skill of husbandry into high art. Contrary to popular misconception, this is not the manipulative wooing of potential husbands: it is the essential talent of carefully managing her diminutive budget.

Extravagance to her is a dirty word unless of course it implies giving in and buying that delicious designer dress she saw in Brown's window. It's not *her* fault it happened to be made by a designer, she tells herself. Even though she can't afford it, she'll find the funds somewhere and tell herself she needs it so as not to show up her husband or boyfriend.

Fortunately for NP woman competition with her rich counterpart is not formidable. The ratio of the nouveaux pauvres to the anciens riches is now so great it's the NPs who dictate fashion. Also the anciens riches are only too happy for an excuse to dress down. British upper-class woman, unlike her European sister, is not obsessed with high fashion and the latest in stylish accessories. While in Paris and Milan the bottom sartorial line for the upper-class woman is Yves St Laurent or Georgio Armani, back in Britain tweeds and gumboots suffice in the country and Laura Ashley and Benetton in town.

Ready-to-wear is almost *de rigueur* among the female upper crust. Too much couturier made-to-measure is regarded as perhaps a little showy and really more the province of flashy film stars.

THE OLDER NP WOMAN

The older NP woman cunningly concentrates on her appearance 'from the waist up' rationalizing that at a sit-down dinner no one is interested in how her skirt clings. Her rule is that to be practical (a necessity she finds more a delight than a burden) an item must be classical rather than fashionable. Hemlines and colours remain constant season after season. Let her lower-class sisters (or her daughter) throw good money after bad on the latest clothing trend. To her, an item is not practical if it doesn't look expensive. She'll skimp and save to be able to fork out for something quite costly like an Hermes scarf or a good handbag which she feels will compensate for an otherwise inexpensive outfit.

NP older woman looks good through judicious mixing. She has one or two really dazzling items to flaunt occasionally. She'll offset a Marks and Spencer skirt with a Jean Muir jacket (splurged on at a Lucienne Phillips sale). A silk blouse from the designers' floor at Harvey Nichols will detract from a nondescript pair of trousers.

For a formal occasion like Royal Ascot NPs will buy for instance a black and cream hat from Marks and Spencer. 'The quality of their straw is wonderful,' says Her Majesty's cousin Lady Elizabeth Anson. 'A similar hat from Freddy Fox costs over £180. The ones at M & S are only £14. And once I dress it up no one will know where I got it.' Perhaps the skill is genetic: 'My mother was once voted "Best-dressed woman of the year" and she dressed at C & A!' reveals Lady Elizabeth.

THE YOUNGER NP WOMAN

The young NP woman retains the airs of her mother's generation. Whatever she wears, she carries it with a lanky grace and casual confidence, thus distinguishing herself from those who are either trying too hard to look good and those trying to look bad.

She may not be a trend-setter but she is a trend-adapter. She cannot afford the Kenzos and Josephs of the world but she can browse through their shops then go and find the closest copy on the King's Road. She'll seldom go wild in her sartorial style – she wants to get invited to polo matches as well as pop concerts. She straddles a fine line between haute couture and proletariat post-punk. In so doing she is recognizable to members of her own group only: she is seen as different by those who subscribe to high fashion as well as to those who garb themselves in 'alternative fashion'.

Fashions move too fast to be able to itemize her wardrobe. A current vogue is the 'breakfast to breakfast' look which is a black dress that can be worn with a whole range of accessories. The other is the 'Easter bunny' look which is a childhood reversion to primary-coloured shapeless dungarees. An NP girl is the one who might wear her brother's jacket with the sleeves rolled up with a shirt from Chelsea Girl and trousers from Monsoon. What these different NP girls' wardrobes have in common is that they don't cost much.

BAUBLES

Because of its sentimental value, jewellery is one of the last of the heirlooms to be cashed in. NP woman still retains a few 'splendid pieces' which she mixes judiciously with plastic bangles, wooden beads and other unassuming costume jewellery. But the Castellani brooch on her bosom declares that the tat she is wearing is 'purely fun'.

She counts herself lucky that she doesn't live in the reign of Charles I who forbade the wearing of imitation jewellery. Instead she wallows in the smug satisfaction that the Princess of Wales put her stamp of approval on tat ever since she first went on a spree at Ken Lane jewellers in Beauchamp Place where she bought £200-worth of baubles for her honeymoon (£200 buys a lot at Ken Lane). And when she was pictured on the cover of a woman's magazine, perceptive NP women noted with delight that she was wearing her £6 Ken Lane earrings.

In fact a thirty-second browse from the Princess of Wales is worth as much to a shop as the Royal Warrant. Any time she steps into a lesser jeweller or boutique, word moves swiftly round the NP circuit: 'Haven't you heard? POW shops there!' This news is less a revelation than a confirmation that NPs were doing the right thing all along.

MAKE-UP

Unlike her middle-class sister, NP woman doesn't rate cosmetics too highly. Mother always taught her to apply just enough make-up to enhance her natural attributes. She also feels (rightly) that upper-class men don't fancy girls with the Dallas/Miss World Availability Look. 'Too much make-up can make a girl look a tart, even if she's as pure as driven snow,' says NP Camilla Scott, a fashionable London model.

So NP woman is rarely seduced into paying through the nose for expensive brands of make-up. Boots No 7 and No 17 ranges have never failed her in either quality or colour selection. The only time you'll find older NP woman swanning round Harrod's Perfumery is when she is lunching nearby. She'll grandly march from one counter to the next, dousing herself with Miss Dior here and dabbing-on Lancome blusher there. Then she'll depart, well made-up for lunch and convinced she's doing the right thing sticking with Boots.

In London, the social NP woman will occasionally splurge on Yves St Laurent lipstick. This is not because she thinks it better than any other, but rather because with its unmissable gilt cover and preposterously large YSL logo, it makes her feel she's keeping her end up when competing with arriviste women at Annabel's Ladies.

SHOES

Her shoes come in three categories: the good; the bad; and the beautiful. The good shoes are classics which she buys in the summer, then dyes dark blue or black for the winter. The bad are not really bad . . . but neither are they good or beautiful. Lady Elizabeth Anson has a pair from Marks and Spencer's which she claims are 'the most comfortable' pair she's ever owned. The beautiful come from a shop like Manola Blahnik or a chain like Bally 'for special occasions only' and are meant to last a lifetime. They would, if only these special occasions didn't keep cropping up!

UNDERWEAR

'I don't know one of my friends who doesn't get all her knickers at M&S,' says a prototypical country NP woman. She doesn't know what to make of those women who spend £30 or more on the skimpy lace jobs. NP man does. The sensuous London NP woman thinks it's worth the splurge and men who get to know her intimately say she has at least two Janet Reger lace knickers amongst her many M&S.

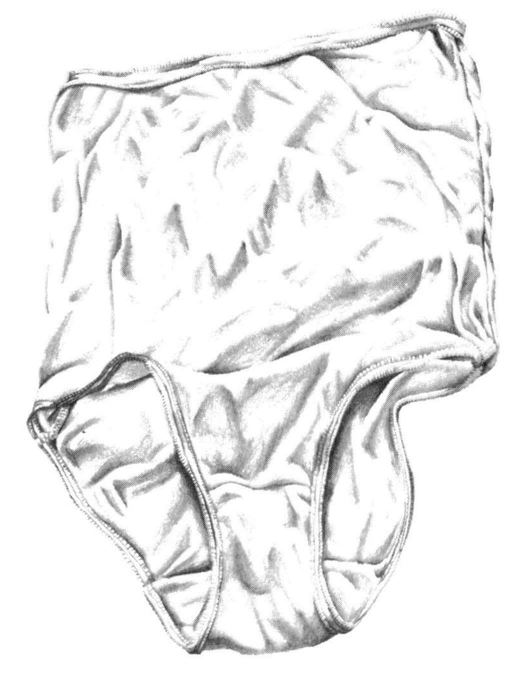

HAIR

The Ancien Riche lady, unbridled by vulgar economies, will visit her hairdresser twice a week. Of course, many don't go merely for the trussing of locks, but rather for the gossip. London's hairdressing network is a veritable databank of scandal that often makes Nigel Dempster's exclusive revelations read like the Court Circular.

Under the fingertips of a favourite crimper, a lady will divulge intimate secrets she'd never dream of telling her priest or psychiatrist. When these self-same ladies are demoted to NPdom, they find the habit of confessing titillating trysts to their stylist hard to kick – especially when they are drawing *out* from the databank. If a true addict, she will stick with the costly crimper, even if it means her dark deeds are a secret held between her blow dryer and Carmen curlers for the two months spanning each affordable visit. Antoine, her neighbourhood hairdresser, might treat her hair adequately. He may even be a third of the price. But Antoine's ears are not so sympathetically tuned as those of Ricci Burns or Leonard.

If gossip-mongering is not the quintessential motive of her visit, there is another reason the NP woman retains the services of the highly priced salon. She is convinced (in marked contrast to her usual practicalities) that her outrageous bill reflects not so much the tiled interior, nor even the inflated rent, but the indisputable quality of the cut. She is not about to put her precious mane in the scissored hands of Antoine. However she doesn't mind him setting it or putting it up for a 'minor ball' or other 'insignificant' event.

How NP women save a Bit Extra on their hair:

When going to Antoine's she'll wash her hair in the bath first, saving herself untold shampooing costs.

▪

Though she wouldn't dare use the above ploy at her upmarket salon, she wouldn't be above forgoing conditioner to save herself a pound. She would have washed and conditioned it the evening before with a cheap brand of conditioner.

▪

She'll go to the expensive salon on 'juniors' night'. There is not much to worry about here as experienced stylists hover nearby, at the ready to prevent any mishaps.

APPEARANCE-SAVING PLOYS

BOP SWAP An example of how the upper classes are coping with their reduced circumstances is well illustrated by the antics of officers' wives in a certain distinguished British regiment. Upon examining the annual regimental ball photographs taken over the last five years observers will notice that each of the wives is wearing a different ballgown from the year before. Upon further examination, it transpires that the same dresses appear in each photograph . . . though on varying wives. They have simply been swapped!

UNHUMBLE JUMBLE SALES London-based NP women haunt Belgravia and Knightsbridge jumble sales hoping to get this season's cast-offs from her more discerning nouveau riche counterpart. More industrious country NPs actually organize the jumble sales themselves, strategically calling upon the houses of rich acquaintances for donations. The best method is to work in a team with a fellow NP from another county. Each siphons off the best designer hand-me-downs and gives them to her partner – thus avoiding the humiliation of encountering the past owner while attired in her expensive Jasper Conran.

TARTING UP TAT NP women can only dream about wearing a ballgown from the likes of Chatelaine or Belville Sassoon. She may moon in front of the windows getting ideas but she will end up somewhere like Wakefords where she can find similar dresses made in synthetic fibre at ten per cent of the price. The clever NP woman buys it then sews on a silk border and if suitable wears a silk sash and bow round the waist. Such a device goes a long way to redeem the most frumpy of frocks.

FROCK-BINS The day before a grand party finds many a desperate NP scurrying from one second-hand clothing store to the next. These dustbins of the wealthy are the ideal providers for NP woman. Inherently practical, she lets no bothersome emotions like shame or pride dissuade her from acquiring these rejects of the rich. After all, doesn't she live with second-hand furniture (antiques) herself?

Tatler columnist Alexandra Shulman says she saw three other guests buying second-hand evening gowns in the Portobello Road on the morning of a dance given for the marriage of Lord Neidpath and Miranda Guinness. Perhaps as many other attenders of this grand dance would have been found at The Dress Box in Cheval Place in Knightsbridge. But they would have had to have been richer. Many of the shop's nob-soiled dresses cost upwards of £1,000 when new. At even quarter that price (the usual rate for The Dress Box) they are beyond the pockets of a lot of NPs.

HAND-ME-DOWNS There now exists a sophisticated inter-network of charity among NP women. This equitable system starts with a rich sister or close friend handing down to her NP beneficiary last season's clothes who in turn does the same all the way down the line. In this way everyone gets the pleasure of giving and only the richest miss the joy of receiving.

UPPERWEAR PARTIES The lower middle classes have their Tupperware parties; but NPs have their 'upperwear' where discarded Yves St Laurent, Kenzo, Cerruti and Jasper Conran exchange noble bodies at a fraction of their retail price.

The phenomenon started in the late seventies when Lady Serena Andrew, the Earl of Bradford's sister, combined a party for her friends with a sale of her frocks 'because', she says, 'I was broke'.

Her friends, some of whom were not so rich either, were delighted to pick up designer clothes at bargain-basement prices and persuaded her to throw another upperwear party so they could add to her dress rails some of their own redundant Georgio Armanis and Calvin Kleins.

'I first started handing out cards for my sales at Ascot. Some people were very disparaging and others thought it quite jolly. Now it's a common phenomenon and everyone accepts it,' she says.

On Lady Serena's guest list there are some names the public would not normally associate with concepts such as 'economy drives' and 'second-hand clothes'. 'A lot of my clients, especially the ambassadors' wives, would be extremely embarrassed if their names were revealed,' she says.

Many of Lady Serena's original clients, like Vanessa Llewelyn, niece of the Duke of Norfolk and wife of the celebrated nightclub impresario Dai, occasionally go off on their own now and flog not only frocks but a whole range of wholesale-priced *objets d'art* – ivory boxes, bangles, mother of pearl picture frames and shagreen – much of it bought from David Wainwright, an adventurous ex-public-school entrepreneur with teams of craftsmen in the Philippines and India.

Lady Serena Andrew. *PHOTO: JODY BOULTING*

Some NPs, however, feel pangs of guilt at selling the garments they once upon a time disposed of at church jumble sales to help prop up some crumbling steeple. Lady Serena now prints on all her invitations that a collection will be made for some specified charity. Whatever the state of their bank balances, NPs never forget *noblesse oblige*.

*

Even the mega-rich are feeling the pinch. At Chelsea Manor Street's Chatelaine, an upper class dress shop, the manager says that *some* duchesses have been ordering a mere four, rather than five, ball gowns per season.

*

MY LITTLE WOMAN 'The little woman' is one of the few ways the NP woman can ever afford to follow the expensive whims of fashion. The identity and address of this appallingly paid seamstress is a close secret usually held by a few family members. Making dresses for their grandmother since the forties, 'my little woman' still loyally knocks out frocks from *Vogue* patterns for daughters and nieces, charging a price that might just have been equitable in the early sixties.

LONDON'S SECOND-HAND CLOTHES STORES

The stores don't actually buy clothes. They just sell them for the owner, taking a cut of approximately twenty-five per cent. But the NP wishing to discard some of her wardrobe at these 'nearly new shops' or 'dress agencies' should bring in only her best designer items as many of the staff seem to derive a sadistic relish turning down lesser frocks. Should her clothes be deemed worthy of resale, they will hang them for up to six weeks. If an item hasn't been sold it gets marked down. If, after another two weeks, there is till no interest, the NP will have to collect her rejected couture or agree to it being sent to Oxfam or some other needy charity.

The Dress Box: 6 Cheval Place SW7
Dress Pound: 125 Notting Hill Gate W11
Dinah Lee: 156 Hammersmith Road W6
Frock Exchange: 450 Fulham Road SW6
Pamela: 93 Walton Street SW3
Pandora: 54 Sloane Square SW3
Sign of the Times: 17 Elystan Street SW3
Tamarene: 57a Blandford Street W1

Buying British

One NP woman was overheard at a drinks party loudly proclaiming that she would 'only buy clothes by a British designer'. Two days later she was sighted by an NP woman who had just put a one-off French designer dress into Dress Box. Guess what the NP was wearing?

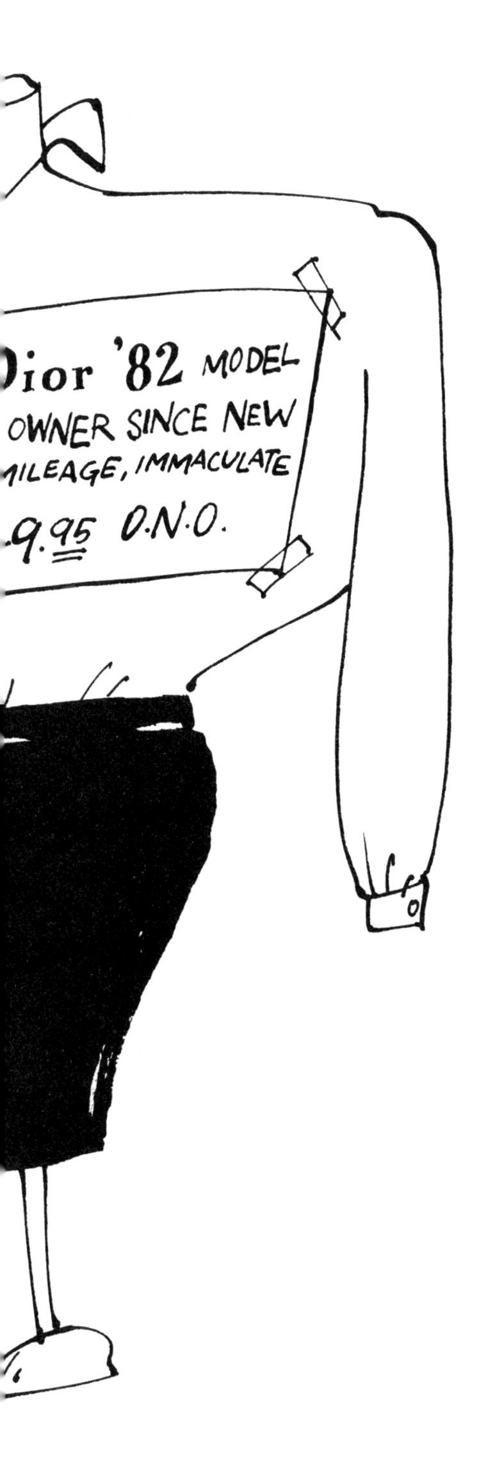

SOME IMPORTANT NP SHOPS

Benetton's: Discovered by NPs *before* Princess Di launched it into the press.
The Warehouse: Great for dungarees but NPs find it difficult to locate natural fibres in some of the other items.
American Classics: For that (hopefully) made-to-measure fifties Hollywood black cocktail dress.
The Liberated Lady: She pops in before a party for fishnet tights and cheap stilettos.
Johnsons: Leather bomber jackets and fun accessories.
Next: She paws through the racks, then complains: 'I never seem to find anything I like here!'
Covent Garden Market: Silly hats and fur pieces to drape around her.
Top Shop: Cheap accessories.

IMPORTANT SALES

Manola Blahnik: Beautifully sculpted court shoes.
Liberty: Fabric for her 'little woman'.
Jaeger: Good skirts that will last a generation.
Alternative Clothing Sale: (Bi-annually at Chelsea Town Hall) She saves shoe leather when all these young designers' wares go on sale under one roof.
Laura Ashley: For that flowered blouse and nightie for country weekends.
The Scotch House: She gets there early for the pick of the cashmeres.
Harvey Nichols: Dior tights and Cacharel blouses.
Lucienne Phillips: Hopes to get a 'bargain' for under £200.
Harrods: Everything.
The British Designer Sales: Organized four times a year at the Rembrandt Hotel, Knightsbridge. Brand-new samples, end of line etc. going at a quarter of, and sometimes under, retail price.

RELATIONSHIPS

SEX: KEEPING A STIFF UPPER ZIP

The price of sex in today's world is often beyond the limits of the NP's dwindling endowment. Peter Townend, social impresario of the deb scene, encapsulates the dilemma astutely. In the past, he says, upper-class young girls were taken out to a restaurant like the Ritz and on to a glamorous nightclub nearly every night of the week when they were not attending a dinner party. 'Nowadays they are lucky to get taken to a pizza parlour,' he remarks. Townend blames restaurants' astronomical prices, yet most restaurants have kept their prices at a level pegging with inflation. The hard fact is that upper-class men's buying power has become impotent.

The ideal upper-class romantic evening should correspond closely to the following scenario: a bottle of Veuve Clicquot in one hand and a dozen long-stemmed roses in the other, young blade Crispin Krugerrandy arrives at the Eaton Square flat of his inamorata Zara Thousand-Acres. After a casually downed glass or more, he whisks her off in his BMW to a seductive, esoteric restaurant like Nikita's where they sip fruit-flavoured vodkas and nibble Beluga caviar. After dinner, he suggests stopping at Tokyo Joe or Tramp, or perhaps some louche dive round the corner where they might be offered a line of cocaine by a generous pop star. Reinvigorated, they stop off at Annabel's where Krugerrandy spends the rest of the evening wondering whether Zara is likely to initiate the move that will make her an honorary member of the Annabel's 'Under the Table' club. Then with requisite formality: 'You simply must see the Augustus John portrait of my grandmother,' he entices her in to his Cheyne Walk penthouse. Reclining on a Louis Quatorze chaise longue, he pours her an age-old cognac then smoothly runs his fingers along her thigh. Coaxing him on, she guides him to the sheer panels of her Janet Reger knickers. Tenderly disrobing her along the way, he leads her to his four poster where, on the cool surface of his Irish linen sheets, they make heady, uninterrupted love for hours.

The typical NP romance takes a different course . . . Hugo Threadbare-Rampant rings Vanessa Yielding-Little and asks: 'Do you mind if I drop by?' He arrives, by underground, at her Parson's Green flat with a bottle of André Simon Vin de Table. Once they've depleted the wine, he assesses the contents of her larder and finding nothing worthy of his palate (i.e. she's run out of baked beans) he announces he's going out to get a kebab. 'Would you like one as well?' he chivalrously offers. Turning out his pockets, he mumbles, 'You couldn't lend me a quid could you?'

If she's lucky, however, he'll take her round to the local Pizza Express where they'll hobnob with fellow NPs, exchanging amusing gossip to the jukebox strains of Siouxsie and the Banshees. Surmising that the tube ride back to Clapham might squelch passion's flames, the wise NP man will wangle his way back to her flat. Upon entering he'll pin her lustily against the wall. As his tongue probes the inner recesses of her ear, she thinks: 'Hell! He's messing up my hair! And I can't afford to go back to Schumi for at least a month.'

As he fumbles with her breasts she considers: 'When should I tell him that my bra is done up with a safety pin?'

As he works his hands down her helpfully gyrating hips, she wonders: 'Am I wearing the knickers with the holes in them?'

And just as Threadbare-Rampant has helped her to find his only hard asset a key is heard in the lock, and Vanessa's flatmate, inadvertently voicing a double entendre, shouts 'Anybody in?' Behind her swaggers the Honourable Dicky Snobcock who, upon eyeing Threadbare-Rampant, drunkenly jokes, 'Damn! One too many for a ménage a trois!'

Discreet negotiations hurriedly take place between the girls and Vanessa takes the flat's one bedroom, leaving Snobcock and quarry in the drawing-room. The spontaneity shattered, the frustrated Hugo none the less wastes no time in dashing Vanessa onto the Jonelle duvet. To avoid displaying their uninspiring M & S underwear, the light goes on only *after* they undress. Then, feeling like stars on the stage, they grapple and groan under the sixty-watt beam of her anglepoise. So strong from cycling to work, her thighs painfully squeeze Hugo's loins.

Then, as he tries to nudge her over, Vanessa suddenly slides sideways off the twin bed. Chivalrously recovering his maiden in distress, he pursues another erotic tack and kisses his way down her body. Insensitive to her requirements for warmth, he presumptuously imagines the ardour of his kisses a substitute for the unreclaimed duvet on the floor and soon finds he is nibbling frigid gooseflesh.

Forgoing more of this 'pleasure' for herself, Vanessa pulls Hugo on top of her to expedite this amorous encounter because she has to be in the office by nine, unlike Hugo, who is 'between jobs' i.e. unemployed.

Their passions spent, the exhausted couple snuggle into each other's arms. Dozing off, the room suddenly reverberates and they are kept awake for the next hour by the penetrating moans and rhythmic yipping of Snobcock and his amour on next door's creaking sofa.

This squalid state of affairs is bemoaned by NPs, yet there is little they can do about it. The hard fact for the NP is that money is as important to gracious wooing as horses are to polo. The NP man might have charm and beautiful manners but without the financial wherewithal he finds a decorous romance difficult to sustain. And for NP woman, reared on the gooey pap of Barbara Cartland and Georgette Heyer, she can only comfort herself with financial dreams of a dashing latterday Darcy whisking her off to some baronial castle amidst acres of wood and pasture.

THE NEW MONOGAMY

NPs of either sex are grateful at least that fornication is one of the few pleasures that is free. Yet while sex can be easy to come by, NPs like Anthony Eyre, who went to Stonyhurst, often find the cost of romance prohibitive: 'Pursuing the woman you fancy is damned expensive. Yes, a lot of them offer to pay for the taxi ride, sometimes even half the meal. But unless you are very close, accepting these gestures can be counter-productive and kill off the romance. Women want to be entranced by a man. They don't want to know about the vulgar practicalities of that entrancement.'

Money problems, it also seems, breed monogamous relationships: as another NP explained: 'If you have a girl who's fond of you, it is far more sensible to stick with her than to go round playing the field. Sure, there are a lot of girls I really fancy, but why go out and spend £200 you probably cannot afford in the slender hope of initiating a romance?'

It is a trend that Peter Townend deplores: 'These young men and women sticking to the same person and not varying their romances is so *middle-class*,' he sighs. But perhaps money is not the only reason for the New Monogamy. Old Harrovian Martin Leggatt, one of London's more desired bachelors, thinks that many women treat their suitors badly and are unappreciative of their swains' financial sacrifices: 'A lot of men I know feel that the women take it for granted when they are dined at a good restaurant. Often they never ring to thank and seem quite unappreciative that to pay for the meal the man probably has to live off baked beans on toast for the next five days.'

Not all NP girls, however, are insensitive to the financial limitations of their suitors. But being sympathetic can breed other problems, as a well-known upper-class fashion model explains: 'I always offer to pay half when I get taken out because I know how expensive it can be. But the first time round the man usually refuses as he is hoping to impress.' She says: 'The next time you'll get invited to his flat for dinner as obviously he cannot afford to pay so soon for another romantic meal *à deux*. Some girls don't mind this. But I feel that wining and dining in his flat on the second date is creating an artificially intimate relationship. If you then refuse to go to bed with him, he can get frightfully upset. Some men have even had the nerve to demand to know why I don't sleep with them when I have signalled a positive response by coming into their flat in the first place. They usually look hurt when I tell them it was only out of consideration for their wallet.'

Some NP men don't court NP woman at all, labelling her as 'erotically unevolved'. They feel the NP woman's life is so versed in mundane practicalities like lugging her Laura Ashley linen to the launderette that sex for her is just a functional coupling of limbs that serves as a tiresome prerequisite for male companionship and affection. These NP men prefer the sort of woman who spends oodles of money tarting herself up for the bedroom. Unlike her NP sister, the nouveau riche woman spends small fortunes on the accoutrements of sex: intoxicating (as opposed to asphyxiating) scent, suspender belts, stockings and alluring make-up. NP man seldom seems to realize that her voluptuous bank account is just as much an aphrodisiac as her UVA suntanned legs.

It seems to this sort of NP man that before the Princess of Wales was exposed to seemingly endless supplies of money, she was just another gawky upper-class girl. With her new-bought sophistication, she is, to him, a goddess.

The Princess of Wales: from gawky girl to goddess. *PHOTOS: DAFYDD JONES (left); JIM BENNETT/CAMERA PRESS (right)*

MARRYING MONEY

NP man often fancifully visualizes marrying money. Recalling bygone days when beautiful 'dollar princesses' came ashore in droves seeking out titles and estates to invest Daddy's millions in, he harbours a recurring reverie: Imagine . . . No more skulking from creditors! No more undignified bargain-hunting in junk shops! A casual canter over the acres every dawn! The swilling of vintage port every night!

Yet NP Bachelor is not merely a taker. His fantasy would not be half so rewarding without the spectre of his angelic wife gratefully receiving, as her end of the bargain, the benefit of her chivalrous husband's illustrious style, culture, charm, etc.

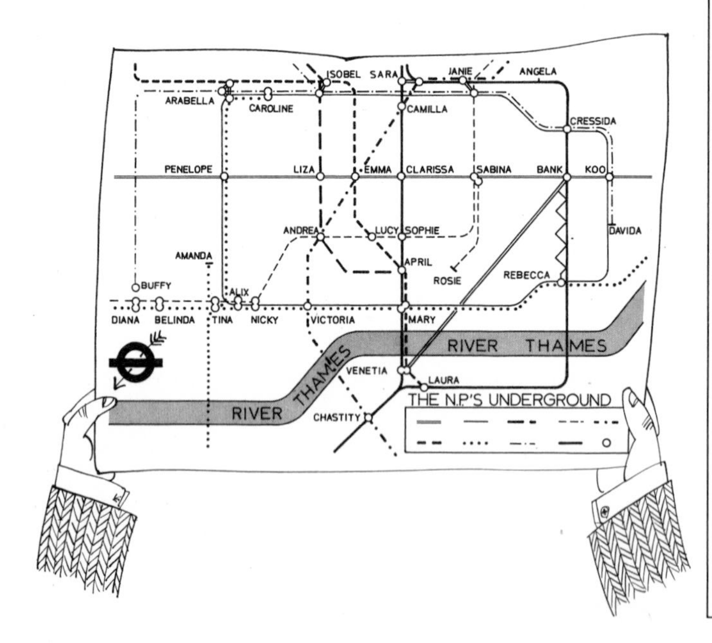

♀♀♀

Unbeknownst to NP man, it is a rare NP girl who has not at least considered the notion of selling her favours. It is seldom morality which prevents her fulfilling her *Belle de Jour* inclination but rather the fear of being found out. One desperately broke NP girl, looking for work in New York, decided to take her chances as she felt a safe 4,000 miles from home. She was introduced to an upmarket madame, who, impressed by the girl's great beauty and style put her straight out *aux asperges*. As she lay in expectant repose on a velvet chaise longue her first customer made his entrance. The NP girl immediately recognized him as a member from the local hunt of which her father was Master. Fleeing through the door, she had learned one quick but traumatic lesson: Don't charge wages for sin when your connections are wide and spread.

♀♀♀

Marrying money, old, new or foreign, was not only respectable for the NP of the past, it was, apart from inheritance, about the only way to re-establish his fortune – trade being beneath his noble station. Sunny, the ninth Duke of Marlborough, loved a poor English girl. Consuelo Vanderbilt loved a fellow American. But both carried responsibilities which transcended the personal. He had Blenheim Palace which needed reroofing and she had a mother whose snobbery needed satiating. Two and a half million dollars later they were hitched. Were they happy? Not particularly, but his palace got a new roof and even after the

'By the third or fourth generation, who'll remember where the regeneration of wealth came from?'

■

– Upper-class justification for marrying money

♂♂♂

Genetically programmed to appease any gnawing appetites, NP man is unused to the restrictions lack of money puts on his life. In the not so distant past when upper-class men were desirous of a purely sexual liaison they were able to slake their lust on courtesans and tarts. Nowadays, on the nights when NP girls have repelled his advances, NP man can neither afford ladies of the street nor dexterous concubines. This is why it is often spoonerishly said that NPs are wally bankers. As one NP man morosely grumbled: 'The biggest deposit I'll ever make is in a sperm bank.'

♂♂♂

divorce he kept the two and a half million reasons why he married her.

But times have changed and with them so have attitudes. For a start, even if NP Bachelor felt there were still beautiful heiresses around, worthy of his marital hand, he suspects that behind them lurk highly protective fathers shrewdly conniving to keep their riches out of the NP's pristine hands. Tragically, the practice of rich fathers-in-law making over small fortunes to their daughters' spouses went out with top hats, he reflects. And another thing, he ruminates, don't the rich tend to intermarry these days? He may be right. As one nouveau riche girl recently said, 'I've got more in common with a racing-car driver than with one of the effete upper classes.'

NPs themselves are actually partly responsible for the downward swing in 'fortunate' marriages. Embracing pervasive middle-class morals, NP Bachelor looks for a suitable girl to love, rather than to replenish his depleted coffers. Even when an heiress with the requisite beauty and charms captures his heart, the modern NP is cautious. Impresario of London's annual deb season and Social Editor of the *Tatler*, Peter Townend, says that many aristocratic suitors have confided to him that they consciously pursue NP women. 'A lot of the more eligible men I know believe that marrying a woman richer than they are invariably ends in disaster. Their fear is that any time there is a domestic squabble, the woman always has recourse to rebuke the husband for living off HER money. The men tell me they couldn't live with that humiliation,' he says. As one NP put it: 'How could you throw a vase at your wife if *she's* bought it?'

'The effort of having a nouveau riche wife is harder than remaining poor,' says one snobbish NP. Not only, he argues, would his upper-class friends and relatives probably ostracize her, but he would have to learn to assimilate into her family and set of friends with whom he's sure he'd have little in common.

In the past, young NPs on the lookout for a 'good match' had the help of their mothers to set up 'fortunate meetings'. But who can arrange such matches today? The deb season has been the traditional marriage market for the upper crust. Currently truncated by diminishing wealth, a threadbare version of this once plutocratic carnival nevertheless continues – though few participate in it for more than a year, of those who do at all. After the age of twenty-one, all but the immaturest of men are too old for the callow girls of seventeen (the average age of 'coming out'). In this progressive day and age by the time either sex is ready to get married, their acquaintances from those fevered, hoolying days are distant memories of a teenage past.

Even when an NP does marry a rich girl today, there can, ironically, be cases where the NP's parents become distraught and try to scupper the match. In spring 1983, Lady Rendlesham tried to dissuade her son, Lord Rendlesham's heir, from marrying the daughter of a retired millionaire hairdresser who had started the chain of Robert Fielding salons. She failed and the wedding went ahead – though not quite as planned. Lord and Lady Rendlesham did not attend.

As an early-nineteenth-century barony, the Rendleshams are undeniably grand, but they are not rich. In the past, such a match between title and wealth would have been blessed as pragmatic. Would Lord and Lady Rendlesham have preferred their heir to be betrothed to another NP, perhaps? Their objection to the union seems historically out of step.

▪

NP WOMAN

NP Woman wants to marry money, but from her own class, thank you. However, competition for the titled *and* rich is fierce. She gets little help from her family as the family lineage was never much affected if the daughter married poor. So the odds are that NP bride will find herself hitched to NP groom. Yet, NP Woman in love is not disheartened by her husband's dim material prospects. She tells herself that her noble betrothed has 'potential'. Precisely where this talent for advancement lies, she is not always sure, but she feels he must have within him *some* of the ignoble traits of pushiness, cunning and opportunism – the compound ingredients for 'getting on'. Behind every Napoleon there's a Josephine, she assures herself as she goes up the aisle, forgetting that by the time Josephine first enchanted Bonaparte, he was already Commander-in-Chief of the French army.

> *From Rags to Riches*
>
> **Perhaps the best means of an NP marketing himself as a marriageable proposition is through hobnobbing with journalists. Somerset silage-pit builder, Lord Kingsale, happened to mention in conversation to Fleet Street diarist Adam Helliker, that he was on the lookout for a rich bride. In no time, this superfluous titbit was featured in the national press. Immediately Breakfast Television followed up the story by inviting a bemused Lord Kingsale to appear on the screen as their guest. With all this exposure, few were surprised when a Dublin millionairess put forward her daughter for marriage to the Premier Baron of Ireland the following week.**

ROUGH DIAMONDS Most NP single girls have their eyes open for the right sort of malleable nouveau riche plebeian. 'If I can catch a sporting one, he just *might* fit in,' she tells herself.

Karen Humphries is an ex-debutante in her early twenties with a horror of following the NP marital path and 'ending up in Fulham – or worse, in Battersea – with a GTI, an estate agent and a Labrador. But that's probably how I will end up,' she laments. 'It is sad, but money *is* so important,' she continues. 'As my friends say, "Better nouveau riche than no riches at all!".' Half jokingly Karen admits what few NP girls would: 'At a party I am often attracted to a charming, handsome, but hopeless, upper-class man – poor as a church mouse. Then I might catch sight of some vulgar, flashy-looking spiv and I find myself thinking: "How quickly could I change him? Make his demeanour more personable? Change his clothes? Make him socially attractive . . . and then marry him?" '

DIVORCE

In a leisurely moment of dilettante scholarship, Lord Kennett recently confirmed the worst fears about the moral decrepitude of the once ruling classes. He calculated that the divorce rate among dukes is thirty per cent higher than the rest of the nation. Divorce is a costly business and there is no greater example of a man who has suffered visibly from its expense than the thrice-married Duke of Newcastle who once resided in a magnificent estate called Clumber Park. His Grace is now blessed with the novel distinction of being the first duke ever to live in a main residence identified by a *number* – a terraced house in Lymington, Hampshire.

Marital stability is evidently not a family trait. The Duke's only sister divorced three times, his oldest daughter twice and his other child Lady Kathleen, is nearly a model of propriety having divorced only once. Her marriage to Ted Reynolds, an underground guard on the Central Line, lasted three days. A relation was heard to observe at the wedding: 'I know it is a tradition for the aristocracy to marry the Guards, but in my day it was the Coldstream or the Grenadiers!' Lady Kathleen was last heard of working as a waitress in a Hong Kong nightclub.

But fecklessness and inherent degeneracy are not entirely to blame for the high rate of divorce among the aristocracy. According to Sarah Greenwood of the Historic Houses Association, many noble marriages founder because of the nouveau pauvre reality of looking after large, economically unviable mansions: 'Young girls from London often imagine a life of feudal bliss as the wife of a country squire,' she says. 'When the bleak and depressing truth dawns upon them that they are engaged in an endless battle against damp, dry rot, draught and usually overdraft, many divorce and return to London, leaving the ex-husband even less financially equipped to survive than before.'

EDUCATION

Education: In holidays from Eton.

■

Sir Osbert Sitwell's entry in *Who's Who*

Legal & General recently calculated that the cost of a child is £70,000. But the requirements for a child born into the 'upper' echelons are greater. With Legal & General's assistance we have computed the costs of providing for a 'well-brought-up' boy or girl. As seen in the following table, either costs the parents until she or he is twenty-one years of age, over £160,000. However the rest of the chapter shows where NPs have learned to compromise in the patrician upbringing of their noble heirs.

COST OF ARISTO

FIRST YEAR		BOY	GIRL	BOTH
Layette, cot and pram				£1,000
Private delivery and consultations beforehand		£2,000	£2,000	
Clothes		£600	£600	
Nanny		£3,000	£3,000	
Food		£400	£400	
Creams, nappies, doctors, medicine, inoculation etc.		£800	£800	
Toys and presents		£200	£200	
	Total:	£7,000	£7,000	£1,000

ONE to FOUR (inclusive)		BOY	GIRL	BOTH
Clothes		£2,400	£2,400	
Food		£1,600	£1,600	
Nanny (girl is born one year after boy, so they share)				£12,000
Presents: tricycles, dolls etc.		£1,200	£1,200	
Holidays		£2,000	£2,000	
Doctors and dentists		£800	£800	
Kindergarten (from two to four)		£3,000	£3,000	
	Total:	£11,000	£11,000	£12,000

FIVE to ELEVEN		BOY	GIRL	BOTH
Clothes, school uniform etc.		£4,200	£4,200	
Food		£2,800	£2,800	
Nanny				£15,000
Holidays		£7,000	£7,000	
Special lessons: piano, swimming etc.		£1,000	£1,000	
Presents and pocket money		£3,500	£3,500	
School fees for boy: Eaton House (5 to 8)		£5,000		
Dragon School (9 to 11)		£9,000		
School fees for girl at Francis Holland School (5 to 11)			£9,000	
Books and stationery		£3,000	£3,000	
Doctors and dentists		£1,500	£1,500	
	Total:	£37,000	£32,000	£15,000

TIC CHILDREN

TWELVE to SIXTEEN

Clothes	*£3,000*	*£3,000*
Food	*£2,000*	*£2,000*
Presents and pocket money	*£5,000*	*£5,000*
Holidays	*£5,000*	*£5,000*
School fees for boy: Dragon School (12 to 13)	*£3,000*	
Eton (13 to 16)	*£16,000*	
School fees for girl: Benenden (11 to 16)		*£24,000*
Recreation (shooting and riding)	*£2,000*	*£2,000*
Doctors and dentists	*£1,500*	*£1,500*
Books and stationery	*£2,500*	*£2,500*
Total:	*£40,000*	*£44,000*

SEVENTEEN to TWENTY-ONE

Clothes	*£3,000*	*£3,000*
Food	*£2,000*	*£2,000*
Allowance for spending money (fun)	*£5,000*	*£5,000*
Holidays	*£7,500*	*£7,500*
Shooting and riding	*£2,000*	*£2,000*
School fees: (boy) Eton for one year	*£4,000*	
University and living allowance (three years)	*£15,000*	*£15,000*
Tour of Australia for nine months	*£5,000*	
School fees of girl Benenden (one year)		*£4,000*
Winkfield for one year (becomes cordon bleu cook, learns how to type etc.)		*£6,000*
Driving lessons then a car each as present (on getting licence)	*£4,000*	*£4,000*
Books and stationery for last year of school and university	*£2,000*	*£2,000*
Doctors and dentists	*£1,500*	*£,1500*
Total:	*£51,000*	*£52,000*

TOTAL COST OF BOY: £160,000
(inclusive of shared cost of nanny & layette etc.)

TOTAL COST OF GIRL: £160,000
(inclusive of shared cost of nanny & layette etc.)

TOTAL COST OF TWO UPPER-CLASS CHILDREN: £320,000
This does not, however, include the cost of the girl's 'coming out' dance, the boy's 'coming of age' and the girl's wedding. This would make the total cost nearer £340,000.

THE BOY'S EDUCATION

It is not uncommon for NP man to hear the heartwarming news that his next child is due to be born precisely when he had thought he had come to grips with his wretched financial situation. Feigning joy, he inwardly calculates how much the new holder of the family name will require. He prays that it's a girl because, despite the nuisance of worrying about her cavorting with yobboes, it has become quite 'acceptable' to send girls to the local comprehensive, though whether he thinks he ever would is another matter. But if it's a boy the first thing that must be done is to 'put him down' for the father's old school.

Public schools are not cheap. A private education for one boy alone will cost him an extra £55,000 (1983 prices). This is a particularly sore point with most NPs who blame the 'outrageous cost of school fees' for their present plight. Yet it never occurs to the NP father to begrudge his boy the same education that he had. Anyway, he reasons, public schools develop character and isn't that aristocratically nurtured trait needed in these dire days more than ever? They also build minds and bodies, though not necessarily in that order. And aren't the rigours of sports vital preparation for life in middle management or wherever the NP son's sorry fate will take him a generation from now? The concept of 'fair play' must still exist *somewhere* in the sanctum of the market-place, he tells himself.

Anyway the latest released results speak for themselves. Only fourteen per cent of state-educated students get 'A' levels compared to fifty per cent in the private sector. And so what if the boy is a dunce? He still gets plugged into a cultural bank that can serve him the rest of his days, irrespective of whether he enjoyed or hated his time at school. However far he falls, he will always belong to the upper-middle-class tribe – though how that will actually make a practical difference to him if he is thrown out on to the street, the NP father is not altogether sure. It just has to be right, he will conclude. After all, it made me what I am – an argument the irony of which rarely strikes him.

The NP father might not, however, remain quite so convinced about educating his son at the best schools an overdraft can buy if he considered some of the disadvantages.

There are many who now argue that the money an NP father spends on educating his children privately would be better spent invested as a nest egg to help set them up when they are adult. Others argue that if they do have their children privately educated they should not be sent to the *best* schools. It is unfair, they say, to groom a boy for a Rolls-Royce existence, when, at the end of the day, he won't have enough money for a second-hand Mini Metro.

Old Etonian Simon Craven is one of that opinion. He is a second-generation NP who says parents should not send their son to one of the elite independent schools unless the family can afterwards afford to support him in a lifestyle commensurate with the expectations a top establishment inevitably cultivates – this rules out all NPs.

'At school I belonged to Pop,' (Eton's prefect elite) he says, 'and I suppose I must have had fanciful illusions about my future, despite being conscious of my family having no money. But it is understandable when you belong to a small privileged group in arguably the most famous school in the world.'

After school Craven found he was quite unprepared for the shock of 'plunging into virtually penniless and sudden anonymity'. Unsuited for the City, he got a job in a record shop. 'The money I earned was just enough to support me in a bedsit. At nights I always had to stay in because I didn't have enough money to go out. I resented terribly not being able to keep up with my old schoolfriends who used to eat out regularly at restaurants and go to nightclubs.

'At school it was bad enough being a poor child among richer ones, psychologically carrying your parents' stigma of financial failure. But if you are bred to be a racehorse and you end up having the duties of a donkey, it is a waste of expensive training. Unless you are exceptionally talented, it can take you years to get a high-earning job in the market-place. I think it is an unnecessary cruelty to give someone expectations of a lifestyle he has little chance of achieving.'

Like many others, Craven thinks that most of the 'top' public schools fail to equip their pupils to cope with the practicalities of money and commerce. 'At school it was vulgar to talk about such things. The public-school ethos is designed to create moral, decent and trusting gentlemen. Boys thus emerge with all the wrong instincts for getting on – a willingness to accept people at their word, a reluctance to be pushy – a recipe for failure in today's world.'

ETON

Traditionally regarded as the Rolls-Royce of public schools, Eton has now come to be regarded by some of the more embittered NPs with the same disdain in which they hold the once-beloved motor car: 'It can't be that good if the Queen chose to send her sprogs to some barracks over the border,' they muse cynically. Yet most NPs still want to give their sons the privilege of having been to Eton, as much for their job prospects as the inherent value of the education. The old-boy network, some reckon, still operates as Britain's most effective employment agency.

But does it? In these meritocratic days many feel the advantage of an Eton education is cancelled out by its disadvantages. Eton might have an undeniable cachet but where lies admiration lurks envy. To a Belgravia hostess, the prototype Etonian is a charming well-groomed gentleman. To the man in the street he's more likely a toffee-nosed git. Breeding and pedigree win out in the drawing-room but they don't necessarily commend you in the office. So for every OE who breaks into merchant banking another is rejected by the more socially hostile manufacturing industries. Where some find that their Etonian background impresses an American client others find it no longer helps to secure a place in a Tory Cabinet – or other such sanctums now dominated by grammar-school graduates.

The traditional supporting base of elitist friends has been eroded too. 'Once you leave

The 'Old Elephants' whose present team includes Kel Gibson-Watt – a constable on the Hammersmith beat.

Eton's cloistered environment, it's difficult enough holding a job yourself, let alone trying to help more hopeless schoolmates,' says one OE. Indeed many Old Etonians feel so embarrassed about their school's elitist connotations, that in the company of more humble folk they go to great efforts to disguise them.

Ex-Captain of the Old Etonian football team Charles Barber relates a story about a match played on Hackney marshes. Finding himself a man short he was relieved to be approached by a local lad offering to make up the numbers. 'Who am I playing for?' he asked as he donned his football gear. 'The OEs,' responded Barber, clearing his throat with some embarrassment. 'What does OE stand for?' the new player awkwardly persisted. Still not wanting to admit the truth Barber answered desperately: 'The Old Elephants, of course.' To the dismay of the team and the bemusement of the spectators, the new player spent the game tearing up and down the left wing shouting enthusiastically, 'Come on you Old Elephants!'

MINOR PUBLIC SCHOOLS

Most old-fashioned NP parents think the idea of sending their boys to a minor public school to play conkers with the sons of rich yobboes absurd when for the same fees they could go to a distinguished major public school to do the same with heirs of viscounts and dukes.

Among a minority of NPs though, there is a new way of thinking on this matter. For a young man setting out in life – a young man with little money – who is more useful to have as a close schoolfriend, they ask themselves:

the heir of a duke whose influence extends over a few miles of windblown Inverness heather or the only son of a cockney entrepreneur with three canning factories in Milton Keynes?

Yes, undeniably it is grand for a young fellow to be steeped in ancient tradition, to have his name chiselled alongside his great-grandfather's in the shadow of a flying buttress and to have imbued in his noble mind an aversion to the vulgarities of commerce. Yet, these NPs ask themselves, isn't it more appropriate for their boys today to rough it with well-heeled tradesmen's sons, understand the way they think and how they work? One successful businessman who is also an aristocrat puts the fortunes of his career entirely down to his minor-public-school background: 'My father put me down for Eton too late so instead I was sent to Uppingham. By the time I left I had scores of business contacts but more than that a shameless relish for making money. I don't think I would have emerged like that from Eton,' he says.

The grander schools, or so these NPs think, have lost touch with what Britain has historically always been – a nation of shopkeepers. Could it be that minor public schools will rise in status as Britain's answer to Fontainebleau and Harvard Business School?

THE FIVE-YEAR PLAN

To combat the crippling costs of private education, many NP parents have begun to subscribe to the idea of a 'privstate' education. Privstate (pronounced with a long 'i') education is a compromise between the NP's aspirations for his child and the immutable thinness of his wallet. Under this plan, NP children get both private and state education. Here's how the five-year plan works: Till a child is ten or eleven, he attends a state primary school. Then he is sent to private boarding school where he is academically crammed to pass Common Entrance. Two and a half to three years later, the boy returns home one holiday from Harrow, having taken his 'O' levels. If he is remotely like ninety per cent of other adolescents he will make a refrain not dissimilar to this: 'Oi Dad, uh . . . I'm getting pretty fed up with school. I need some freedom. How about letting me go to the local comprehensive or sixth-form college, eh?'* If he were one of the anciens riches, the father would ignore the request, lightly dismissing it as a facetious whim of rebellious youth. The NP father, however, looks grimly at the apple of his eye, who is shiftily studying the wallpaper to avoid the stern parental gaze, before quickly saying 'Yes' to this miraculous money-saving scheme. After all, muses the father, now that young Crispin has spent three years at Harrow, he will always belong to that select club of 'Old Harrovians' and at half the cost.

* Typical rebelspeak, which most public schoolboys at some time adopt. V. sensible as an upper- and middle-class accent can excite hostility among other teenagers and others who should know better (see 'Accent' and 'The Lorraine Walker Syndrome').

THE GIRL'S EDUCATION

The education of their womenfolk has never been one of the more distinguished hallmarks of the British aristocracy. Gels might have been flawlessly bred as chatelaines of their future husband's noble household but an appreciation of the Arts and Sciences beyond the superficial requirements of dinner-party prattle has not traditionally been encouraged: 'Education gives a girl thick ankles!' declared Lord Redesdale to his infamous Mitford daughters.

So when a despondent NP father is informed by his accountant and bank manager that either he remortgages the estate or he cuts his outgoings by £5,000 a year, it is not then surprising that little Sophie's future years of adolescence, once assured at Benenden, come under review.

What does it matter, thinks the NP father, if his girl attends some rough comprehensive and emerges in the hazy belief that Molière is a brand of hair conditioner? If a girl can spell she can qualify as a secretary and if she can't she can always prepare directors' lunches in the City. What good is a degree? Would the Prince of Wales have married Diana 'three-"O"-levels' Spencer if she'd been a bespectacled undergraduate with a concerned interest in Comparative Anthropology or Applied Physics?

But in the end, if sacrifices have to be made, the traditional NP father compromises by sending his daughter to a nearby private day school at forty per cent of the average boarding-school cost. Comprehensives might be free but the thought of a fifteen-year-old Sophie having amorous encounters with louts called Trevor and Kevin is a notion he finds altogether too disturbing to contemplate.

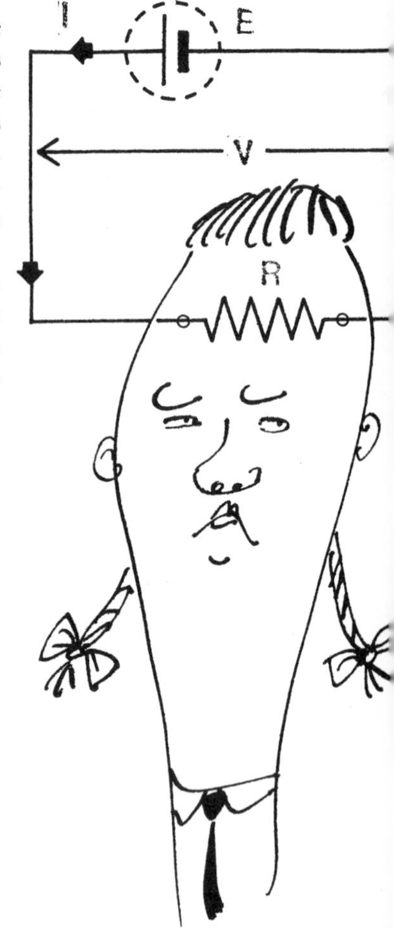

(a) Internal Resistance

$$R = \frac{E-V}{I}$$

R = Resi

E = Educ

V = Ver

I = Intel

GIRLS' PUBLIC DAY SCHOOL TRUST

NP parents hit by bankruptcy or some similar financial unpleasantness while their daughter's still at school, have become keen hunters of local independent schools affiliated to the Girls' Public Day School Trust. These parents, if hoping for a sporting chance to get this organization to subsidize little Camilla's school fees, are advised to demonstrate visibly their dire circumstances. This means they should turn up to the interview on a bicycle and dressed conspicuously in hand-me-downs. Parents are *not* advised to postpone the interview with lines like: 'Sorry we can't make it next week. We'll be skiing in Gstaad.'

In London the two affiliated girls' schools which are most highly rated by NPs are Putney High and Wimbledon High. The most-heard NP rationale for pulling little Camilla out of Roedean to attend one of these schools is: 'Poor thing. We couldn't bear the idea of her stuck away in the country, missing out on all London's got to offer.'

SCHOOL FEES

Faced with a sizeable bill from Eton for a term of his son's education, an NP peer wrote to the bursar and suggested that since he was short of immediate cash could he perhaps provide the college with his forthcoming potato crop? The bursar, fearing no doubt that this could set a dangerous precedent, declined, and the peer had to find the money elsewhere.

For the average family the shock of paying for a private education is second only to that of paying for a house. For the financially unprepared NP, it is often the case that to pay the school fees he has to sell his house.

Most NP children's school fees are paid, in various permutations, by grandparents, parents and a trust. NP parents will make numerous sacrifices to garner the necessary funds for little Crispin to go to school. Foreign holidays and recently registered vehicles are usually the first luxuries to be forsaken. Flogging family heirlooms and decamping from the manor into the gardener's cottage are just some of the more desperate measures which could follow.

Clever parents will approach family relations upon the birth of the NP child and explain to them the benefits of contributing to an Education and Maintenance Trust. Uncle Rupert will listen bemusedly while the NP suggests giving little Crispin yearly instalments of cash. He had no intention of doing anything more than putting down a case of port for the little tyke. But Uncle's ears begin to twitch when NP father explains that Uncle will get sixty per cent tax relief on any funds he puts into the trust. Isn't it marvellous that he could appear so generous when in reality he need only give forty per cent of the amount?

Some NP parents make the mistake of approaching the school directly for financial assistance. Though some independent schools do award grants to the sons of fallen or impoverished old boys (Marlborough and Christ's Hospital take numerous vicars' sons), many schools suggest that the penurious parents give them whatever they can afford, so that the school can invest it for them. Invariably the capital growth on these 'investments' is so minuscule that after the first couple of terms, there's hardly enough funds left over to buy little Crispin a second-hand Latin primer.

However there are companies like SFIA (the School Fees Insurance Agency), which offer numerous schemes to save money out of income, or let it grow out of capital, to pay school fees. The company offers 'years of specialist experience', tax advantages and an annuity to cover the ravages of inflation. But it must be remembered they are in business to profit by the NP's patronage and he could well find other schemes with a higher capital growth elsewhere. Furthermore NPs should beware of the accountant who advises them to partake of such a scheme as his judgement could be influenced by an enticing introductory commission (see 'Do You Trust the Trustees?').

HOW TO USE SFIA Under the various schemes, parents can pay a capital sum in advance, or make annual payments out of their incomes or both. Whatever the case, the sooner the scheme is implemented, the better the returns. Responsible NP parents don't even wait until the christening to put the plan into effect.

The first step parents must take is to determine the total fee costs. Under the SFIA capital payment scheme, if a parent needed to pay fees totalling £15,000 starting in 1988 when little Percival was ready to enter school, and if he had paid a sum of £7,693.70 by 15 August 1983, the full £15,000 would be paid direct to the school by the agency in time for the commencement of his first term. The capital sum is simply invested with the agency, who in turn invest it with an insurance company.

On the income payment scheme the parents (or any other donor) can spread the cost over a period of years, making annual payments out of income. The SFIA claim that when payments are spread over fourteen years, a prep- and public-school education that would normally cost £25,000 would, under their scheme, cost only £14,523 – thus saving the NP parent over £10,000.

Young NP parents can pay out low premiums at first, raising payments as their incomes increase.

CHARITABLE TRUST FUNDS There are a limited number of charitable trusts set up to assist 'deserving' cases in attending independent schools. Certain political parties would like schools outside the state system to lose their charitable status. But as long as these trusts exist, NPs would do well to investigate them. Details can be obtained from The Grants Advisory Officer, Independent Schools Information Service, 56 Buckingham Gate, London SW1.

ASSISTED PLACES SCHEME Much to the delight of NPs the present Tory Government has instituted the Assisted Places Scheme to award part or full independent school fees to needy and bright children. Because it is designed to help those children whose needs cannot be met at their local schools, NP parents, quick to decipher the bureau-babble, have found that for little Crispin and Camilla to qualify they must demonstrate they would both be shockingly deprived if they had to attend a state school where they couldn't take 'O' or 'A' levels in subjects like Egyptology and Swahili. The procedure is not quite as simple as that – NP parents must do their homework and find an independent school that offers such exotic and diverse courses. Then they must convince the headmaster to take the children.

The APS is presently affiliated to over 235 schools (including St Paul's, Westminster and Winchester) and, despite political flak, is due to expand to assist a wider range of students, i.e. not just the bright ones. APS pays on a sliding scale depending upon the family's income and number of children. Most of the children on the scheme come from families whose income is less than £7,500 a year. NP parents who are self-employed, sometimes arrange their affairs so as to qualify for assistance – though the morality of such a ploy is questionable. For information contact: The Department of Education, Elizabeth House, York Road, London SE1 7PH.

■

THE CONVENIENT BOARDING SCHOOL

The most important consideration for NP parents in choosing a boarding school now is geographical location. The NP father might be seriously impressed by the prospectus of Beatemard School in the Yorkshire dales but if he resides in London, he can safely add on another £300 a term in extra travel costs for visiting, i.e. petrol and hotel costs. If it is possible, canny NP parents always choose a school within an hour's driving distance.

The other advantage NPs find in sending their children to a nearby boarding school is the increasingly fashionable practice of certain boarding schools of having weekly boarders. This of course means lower fees.

When the name tags have been sewn into his underpants and the father's old tuck box hauled down from the attic, the NP parents are left with one last worry: will little Crispin make friends with a HAMBRO, CAZANOVE or better still a ROTHSCHILD – or will he foolishly ignore them because they are not as agile at sports as he?

STATE BOARDING SCHOOLS

Some NP parents believe that the better part of education is in the boarding (developing character, midnight raids on school tuck shop etc.). Such parents might be interested then in sending their children to a state boarding school if they lack the funds to despatch them to an independent school. These schools exist primarily for children with an obvious need to go to a boarding school – for example, children from broken homes. These schools are usually located in areas where there are military bases and so can also serve the sons and daughters of troops serving overseas. The state pays for the tuition, which is rated 'jolly good' by many parents, who have only to pay for their children's board and lodging. The future of the state boarding school is in jeopardy as some education authorities are not convinced that they are a good thing. But for NPs who think they are, three of the most highly-rated are: Cranbrook School, Cranbrook, Kent; Wymondham, Norfolk; and Sexey's School, Somerset. All three are co-educational. For further information contact W.H. Spray, Windhover, Manton Down Lane, Marlborough, Wiltshire. Tel: Marlborough 52764.

DAY SCHOOLS

Day schools can save parents over £1,500 a year. However, for a boy to get into a good London school like Westminster or St Paul's he needs to be very bright. Most country public schools discourage day boys as they remain outsiders in the otherwise integrated society of boarders. However, with the substantial savings (approximately forty per cent) that many NPs can make by their children not using the boarding facilities, the practice could soon grow to be quite common.

GRAMMAR SCHOOLS

In 1976 grammar schools were told to turn comprehensive (i.e. open their doors to the masses), turn private or close down. But certain Tory boroughs in the south east of England and some remote rural shires rebelled against this Labour legislation and to this day, 170 grammar schools remain within the state system.

If their children are bright enough, NPs would do well to get them into some of these grammars, whose academic records exceed those of many public schools. Many London NPs sell up and move to a country borough served by a good grammar school. They calculate they save over £35,000 per child in school fees this way *and* they get the academic results.

COMPREHENSIVES

When NPs have no option but to send their children to a comprehensive, they would be uncaring parents if they didn't at least try and get them into the best one in the vicinity. Though compared to independent schools, comprehensives have abysmal examination results, there are some comprehensives whose academic performance is unrepresentatively good.

No doubt the NP will hear much of the respective schools' reputations in the community but he could do worse than examine the brochure that by law all schools now have to provide, giving full details of their curricula and performance. Ignoring the smooth blandishments embroidered into the text of these public-relations efforts, the NP should delve deeper into the headmasters' respective manifestos.

Perhaps it was a right-wing bigot who said that 'the road to educational hell was paved with socialist intentions', but many NP parents judge progressive buzzwords of the late sixties/early seventies as an academic death knell. For a thoroughly biased academic means test of comprehensives, the NP could do worse than follow this procedure: Go through the brochure and add up the words: 'care', 'relevance', 'community', 'culture', 'understanding', 'growth', 'needs', 'imaginatively', 'project work' and 'creative'. Score double if they are italicized or underlined or in capital letters. Next count: 'performance', 'result', 'ability', 'achievement', 'competition', 'motivation', and 'success'. The higher the score of the latter category and the lower of the former, the greater the child's chance of achieving those exam results that will be so vital for him or her later on.

If the NP parents find, however, that all the comprehensives in their borough have unacceptably low academic standards and they cannot or are not prepared to move house, that does not necessarily mean their children are doomed to some educational graveyard. There is a ploy among certain NPs and wised-up middle classes which works in the following way. Provided the children can travel the necessary distances every day, the parents scrape enough money together to buy a short lease on a small residential property – a bedsit will do – in an area nearby which is served by a comprehensive with a good academic record. The property can then be rented out, but, as the registered owners, the NP parents are absolutely entitled, at least legally, to send their children to that school as opposed to any of the inferior ones that might serve their real borough.

SIXTH-FORM COLLEGES

Not to be confused with the academically egalitarian tertiary colleges, sixth-form colleges are very popular with NP parents who subscribe to the Five-Year Plan. Their disadvantage is that the discipline is far more lax than at most independent schools. Students experiencing the whiff of freedom might be somewhat lacking in self-motivation with disastrous consequences for their 'A' level grades, if they get 'A' levels at all. NP parents say that the same criteria apply for choosing a good sixth-form college as a comprehensive. A good sixth-form college can be as good as an expensive crammer. The Solihull sixth-form college has been getting pupils not only good 'A' levels but also Oxbridge scholarships.

THE LORRAINE WALKER SYNDROME

Any NP parents who decide upon a state education for their offspring should beware a common hazard – The Lorraine Walker Syndrome.

Lorraine Walker it was who, in 1978, was dubbed 'Little Miss Posh' by the popular press after a story was leaked about her being persecuted by her fellow pupils at her east London comprehensive because she didn't speak with a strong Cockney accent. What made this news interesting was that one teacher, far from discouraging the bullying of this otherwise blameless girl, allegedly joined in. But instead of the pupils being shamed into desisting from this unrelenting persecution, the publicity aggravated the poor girl's plight. Some of her neighbours, thinking that perhaps the Class War had started in earnest, threw stones at her in the street. Poison-pen letters and death notes were dropped through her letterbox. She was rung day and night with obscene and violent threats. All the while she had to have police protection until eventually she had to leave the area.

It is often the case that sons and daughters of NP parents have to regionalize their accents, if not exactly for survival, certainly for a comfortable life among their fellow pupils. NP parents, however, become particularly distressed when they hear the steady transition from Queen's English to Janet Street-Porter's in their little Hugo and Camilla.

Nor does this brand of knee-jerk class prejudice exist only at comprehensives. Outside the bastions of the upper middle classes, it can be found everywhere. Old Harrovian NP Piers de Laszlo, who is now a successful artist, says the one unpleasant aspect of attending Art College in Camberwell was being subjected to 'snide and tedious inverted snobbery'. He says he could understand it from some of the students who were young and didn't know any better. What surprised him was getting it from the tutors and lecturers.

'I remember one time I entered a student's room at a party. A tutor was in there who said "Don't you think we ought to charge him to come in?" So I asked why. "Because of your rich background," he replied. I then told him he knew very well I had no money. "Yeah," he said "But you act *rich.*"

'It was typical sixties prejudice,' says de Laszlo. 'If you speak the Queen's English these days, it doesn't reflect your material status though it might reflect your values.

'One is allowed to live in a council house, own the latest hi-fi and video equipment, two flashy cars and go for a cruise on an ocean liner every summer and no one discriminates against you for your lifestyle.

'There are a lot of other people who, with the same money, prefer to drive an old banger and live in a rambling country house with a pretty garden and if necessary eat baked beans on toast every day to maintain it. OK. They might speak with a posh accent but that is no grounds to attack them. Class war might have ostensibly been about money once, but now it is about people with one style attacking people with another,' he says.

For most NP students the only effective way to counter the prejudice is to adapt their accents and radically alter their demeanour. It might be alien to them, but at least it spares them the problem of being a focal point for bigotry. So don't be fooled by a young man with a Tyneside accent and a donkey jacket . . . he could be an NP.

UNIVERSITIES

The minimum allowance for a gentleman student in 1832 was thought to be £600 a year (*Life of a Sportsman* by Nimrod). In today's money that is £11,000. The NP is lucky to receive a third of that allowance, but he finds his relative penury little obstacle to indulging in the excesses of his forbears. While they got drunk on good clarets and vintage ports, he gets plastered on cheap Riojas and pungent ales. While they might have gambled hundreds of pounds a night, he will recklessly wager fivers. While they might have gone wenching in Drury Lane, he saves himself the train fare to London and ravishes females on the campus.

The middle-class notion of striving for a good degree is entirely novel to the British upper classes. University was an opportunity for indulgent irresponsibility; serious learning was an incidental afterthought. A display of conscientious study was considered bad form. One either took a first effortlessly or worked just enough to scrape a pass. Anything in between lacked social cachet.

But NPs in today's bleak world know that the class of degree determines not just salary but the chance of getting a job at all. NPs study hard and even then they know it is no guarantee for a niche in the market-place. Grandson of Sir Winston Churchill, Rupert

α, β, б

NPs who come from a long line of Oxbridge scholars have the advantage over those whose grandfathers were more interested in shooting grouse than attending university. It is these, with their handed-down knowledge of the various colleges, who know it is just as easy to get into the bad Oxbridge colleges as it is to get into an anonymous university elsewhere. The point is they have to know which Oxbridge colleges to apply to. Less intellectually committed NPs might find favour with St Edmund Hall, Oxford and Peterhouse, Cambridge.

ψ, ω, Γ

Soames, was President of the Union and a shining star in the firmament of Oxford University, but so many companies turned him down after he left, at one time it seemed he was going to disappear into the black hole of unemployment.

The other crucial difference between NPs and their ancestors is that all the NP's forbears would have gone to either Oxford or Cambridge. But now Oxbridge elitism is academic and only remotely social, few but the cleverest NPs are taken into their ancestral alma maters. Most are destined to attend lesser seats of learning – some even have to resort to polytechnics for their degrees. All these NPs bitterly resent failing Oxbridge. Not for them the indulgence of ancestral illusions amidst skyward gothic monuments. These NPs have to square up to the egalitarian rebuke of acres of loveless red brick – a discomforting premonition, many NPs feel, of a bleak and graceless future. Yet many NPs declare that at least these redbricks do the service of preparing them for the world outside – unlike Oxford or Cambridge. It is the Oxbridge NPs, bathed for three years in an illusory privileged ambience, who find it particularly hard adjusting to the realities of a Clapham maisonette and a badly paid job in a City tower block.

POLYTECHNICS

The NP father is often quite bewildered by the fact that despite his children managing the prodigious feat of getting 'A' levels, they are actually refused entrance to either Oxford or Cambridge. In his day a chap could get into these hallowed seats of learning for boxing or pulling an oar.

'A' level grades are the bane of today's NP students. All too often if examination techniques are not their forte, the best alternative to retaking the dastardly exams is to enrol at a polytechnic. The very word provokes sniggers down the corridors of academe. A polytechnic degree is a chip on the NP's intellectual shoulder for life.

But NPs can take consolation in the statistics. Wasn't Kingston Polytechnic rated higher than thirty per cent of competing universities? Indeed, it was recently put up for university status. Yet what bothers NPs is the lack of a privileged scholastic tradition. At Oxford Polytechnic the NP cannot contemplate the writings of Descartes beneath the gaze of ancient, weathered gargoyles, nor read Aristotle behind leaded windows. The purpose of a polytechnic is to train him for life, not to encourage him to enjoy it. The young NP is aware of this and doesn't resent studying to the light of a bare tungsten bulb reflected off breeze-block. Besides, many NPs continue to live at home while at polytechnic. As far as they are concerned, a polytechnic offers bucket-shop education – university without the frills. It is a bargain many of them can't ignore.

Furthermore, polytechnics provide degrees and diplomas in the sort of practical subjects that universities don't. His ancestors may have been steeped in the Classics, but today's NPs are realizing that a course in

Oceanography or Fashion Design would be better preparation for earning a living. A second in Languages from Bristol University might be impressive, but a second in Business Studies from Central London Polytechnic is a more tempting qualification for a prospective employer. And it's a good job, not intellectual kudos, that the NP is after.

THE GRAND TOUR

In his glorious past, the NP's ancestor would have rounded off his son's education with the 'Grand Tour'. The purpose of the Grand Tour was to inspect the civilized world (i.e. Europe) in a degree of comfort and style (i.e. accompanied by servants), acquire a knowledge of foreign habits (i.e. expensive courtesans), and bring home some souvenirs (i.e. Durers, Rembrandts, Elgin Marbles, etc. etc.).

Just 18, and Old Etonian James Ogilvy prepares to ''travel extensively'' for 12 months before going on to university, here accompanied by father Angus Ogilvy and Henrietta Newman, a friend. *PHOTO: ALAN DAVIDSON, CAMERA PRESS*

This tribal custom of the British upper classes continues, but with some pertinent differences. The last thing an NP father wants is his eighteen-year-old son hanging around, drinking all the booze. 'You must see what's left of the Empire before it's too late,' he declares. The family then inspect a map to see which of Britain's ex-colonies has most family friends and relations. Scoring double if they are rich, they then pick the most suitable corner of the globe. The connections are then written to, with instructions 'to make sure Roland is all right' for the next nine months.

Packed off on a bucket-shop bargain flight, Roland then arrives in Australia, New Zealand, Canada, South Africa or Kenya. The idea is, of course, that Roland pays his way as a menial employee. There are two problems: there is rampant unemployment at the lower end of the job market; and he doesn't have a work permit.

The result is that the long-suffering colonial connections have to support his idle habits, listen to his uninformed views and entertain him while he makes gauche passes at their neighbour's unattached daughter.

After frantically ringing their friends to see if anyone will take 'this charming young Englishman' off their hands, a ranch or sheep farm is located at the back of some rural beyond where Roland is hastily despatched to toil long hours for diminutive wages.

But in future years Roland is grateful for those months of loneliness and alienation. Without that inuring experience how could he possibly stand it so long dwelling in a south London bedsit miles from any tube station?

THE FINISHING TOUCH

Mum probably went to Winkfield where she learned to arrange sweet peas and to prepare Beef Wellington. Finishing schools were the civilized way of breaking in a young lady who didn't know the difference between an omelette pan and a collander. As recently as a generation ago, most upper-class ladies were still sheltered from the harsh realities of what went on in a kitchen and so a formal education in culinary matters was essential if she was to get on in her double role of the age: hostess/housekeeper. ('The daily and the au pair girl can't do *all* the work.')

Finishing schools were the perfect vehicle for them to travel between the luxurious ease of the manorial nest and the new rigours of haute housewifery. Under the expert tutelage of Constance Spry, they could also stall for time until Lord Right came along.

A favourite occupation for horsey NP girls who have flunked their 'O' levels is that of a 'galloping' or 'riding matron' at a girls' prep school. Working long hours at Victorian wages they are more than happy to keep the unruly girls harnessed in return for livery facilities.

Today's NP girls should be practical. Lord Right will, most likely, turn out to be Lord Wrong – in his wallet at least. Instead of preparing to run a stately home, she ought perhaps be trained to manage a pension fund. But NP girls are not interested in careers. A job to tide her over until her wedding day is all she aspires to.

Nowadays she may be sent off to Winkfield, but it is less to learn to arrange her own flowers than it is to qualify for a job as flower arranger. The study of culinary techniques comes in handy when she needs to earn cash by cooking directors' lunches. She learns to type, not so much for her own correspondence on estate matters, but for her spiv boss's property dealings.

Her parents may lend a hand in her education. They groom her to be pretty, gossip discreetly and to be popular. It is better to be a poor lady than a rich woman, they teach her.

The upper-class girl has mostly tended to develop her instincts at the expense of her mind. She may be able to stare down a bolting horse, but she can't tell a Monet from a Munnings. Pretty NP girls, with no qualifications and even less ambition, often forgo further education of any sort and go into modelling.

Some NP girls do go to university. Whereas her American counterpart would use her education to get into investment banking or to enter academia, the NP seeks intellectual and social cachet which will be rewarded with a job in publishing or one of the auction houses. The money she will earn in a year will probably be less than her American cousin's expense account.

Many NP girls go straight into jobs without bothering to qualify formally. Why

ARTISAN COURSES

The Inchbald School of Design
7 Eaton Gate, London SW1
01 730 5508
She'll take a practical course on broken paint technique or garden design.

China Restore Studio
25 Acfold Road, London SW6
01 731 2809
If nothing else, she can finally piece together that old Meissen vase she's been keeping the loo brush in.

The Roger Newton School of Decorative Finishes
12 Allez Street
St Peter Port, Guernsey
0481 28895
She might take the furniture-painting course, but is more partial to the gilding course where she learns the preparation of gesso and laying and burnishing gold.

John Makepeace's School for Furniture Making
Parnham, Beaminster, Dorset
0308 862204
Became famous when Viscount Linley studied here.

West Dean College
Edward James Foundation
West Dean, Chichester, Sussex
024363 301
She studies furniture restoration and other upmarket carpentry courses.

take a course in the history of art when she was nursed under a Velasquez? Anyway, Daddy can always threaten to sell his Van de Veldes elsewhere if Christie's don't put her on the silver counter, she reasons. Art history courses are a bit effete. Practical NP girls would rather take artisan courses. The word 'artisan' implies getting her hands dirty – something NP women have always accepted in trying times. She feels at home with ancient crafts that are dying – rather like her own class. Or she might take a one-year foundation course in fine art which she'll use as a first step before going into interior designing. (Few, if any NP girls become commercial artists.) Though she can take a foundation course at any art school in the country, she goes in numbers to Byam Shaw School of Drawing and Painting, 70 Campden Street, London W8, 727 4711 or 52a Walham Grove, London SW6, 385 5220.

■

Ladies have always been proficient at sewing and flower arranging. Now she gets formally trained and hopes to earn a few bob while indulging in her traditional pastimes.

SEWING

She takes local evening courses in pattern cutting so she can make original designs, or attends the intensive dress-making course run by Mrs Bailey of 18 Pelham Street, London SW7. Many of the fashionable crop of Britain's Young Designers trained at her exclusive establishment.

FLOWER ARRANGING

Constance Spry Flower School
53–57 Marylebone Lane, London W1
01 486 6441

COOKING COURSES

For the NP girl who flunks her 'O' levels and is taken out of school at sixteen, often the only thing she ever qualifies for is cooking. She'll attempt to cover up this deficiency by bragging that she's got a Cordon Bleu Diploma.

Cordon Bleu Cookery School
114 Marylebone Lane, London W1
01 935 3503

Leith's School of Food and Wine
36a Notting Hill Gate, London W11
01 229 0177

THE TOWN RESIDENCE

Not so long ago, the British upper class divided the annual calendar between country seat and London town house. The London abode was a bustling centre of seasonal activity located in St James's, Knightsbridge, Belgravia or Mayfair. Teams of servants went about the humdrum business of announcing distinguished callers, polishing the de Lamarie silver, brushing the Persian rugs, and preparing vast banquets.

The difference between the London life of his forebears and the NP's is not dissimilar to the difference between a ball at the Dorchester and take-away fish and chips in Stepney.

DOWNSTAIRS/UPSTAIRS

Few NPs own a house in those boroughs once patronized by their ancestors. In the smart boroughs of London a fortunate NP might own the tether end of a lease of a converted flat in what all too often was once the claustrophobic confines of the servants' quarters. But more usually, NPs living in the smarter part of the West End are sitting tenants attempting to extort a five-figure sum out of the Grosvenor estate or a Mayfair property company so that they can move elsewhere. When they think they've got the best price, they'll tell their friends they're leaving Mayfair because 'It's swarming with call girls – we call it "Payfare".'

The worst part of the NPs' humilating exodus to London's unsalubrious hinterland is that those who now occupy the spacious apartments of his ancestors are more than likely the direct descendants of his grandfather's valet or worse.

As recently as the late seventies, a few lucky NPs were calling some of the grander rooms at the Ritz 'home', for as little as £5 a day. These opportunists had ingratiated themselves with Mr Ritz and fixed the price when £5 bought more than it does today. No one questioned the right of the old friends of Mr Ritz to be there, that is, until Lord Matthews took over.

In the swinging sixties Chelsea became an NP haven, but today's young NPs can't afford desirable SW3 residences which have escalated to over £250,000 in value. Some NPs, however, inhabit bedsits, minuscule basement flats and fourth-floor eyries with no lifts. They feel they are maintaining their dignity by being able to print letterheads with addresses like Elm Park Gardens, or simply The Vale, SW3.

It is the fringe areas of 'smart' London like SW5 and SW10 that NPs most heavily populate. Earl's Court has had a discernible rise in cachet ever since the Princess of Wales was wooed at Coleherne Court. And opposite at Coleherne Mansions another royal romance upgraded 'Kangaroo Valley' as swarms of paparazzi snapped the comings and goings of Koo Stark. But SW10 is decidedly smarter. NPs living in this buffer zone of World's End between Chelsea and Fulham have the smug satisfaction of having a Chelsea-associated '352' telephone exchange.

Some NPs are pathetically unrealistic about the longevity of their predicament, believing that justice will soon prevail in the form of a rising property market, and consequently duping themselves into buying stamp-sized houses in Fulham and Parson's Green in the mistaken belief that if they followed the example of their industrious middle-class contemporaries, they could start moving up the property ladder with them. Unfortunately for most NPs, ambitious projects like this seldom work for them. Invariably they run out of auctionable items to help on the mortgage repayments and are forced to sell just as the market has been declared a buyer's rather than a seller's market.

But there are NPs who have done well in Fulham – for example, those who bought cheaply in Hurlingham where house prices now run as high as £140,000. Hurlingham residents consequently think they are now very grand. Pointing to the smart new restaurants and shops opening up on the New King's Road these NPs pronounce that SW6 is now as posh as Chelsea – a claim which of course is laughed at by the ancien riche of SW1 and SW3. But it is undeniable that ever since Debrett's moved their offices to SW6, the nouveaux pauvres natives of Fulham have felt a discernible rise in status.

THE GREAT CROSSING

Many London NPs, unable to accept the fact that they have lost their country seat, have compensated, like Earl Alexander of Tunis, by establishing residence in the pastoral communities south of the river. With admirable self-parody they gentrify the names of the different boroughs. Clapham they pronounce 'Clarm', Stockwell and Streatham become 'St Ockwell' and 'St Reatham'. With Battersea they stress all the wrong syllables so it is pronounced like 'Boadicea'. Some even laughingly refer to Battersea as 'South Chelsea'. This is to demonstrate that living there is really quite amusing – not to be taken seriously. It also shows they really do know better: they merely *choose* to live there. Most single NPs actually spend so much time at dinner and drinks parties north of the river that they grow to regard their Wandsworth Common flat as merely a place to store their dinner jackets.

These NPs have developed a highly polished list of rationale for living in these brave new boroughs of London. But lack of money is never one of them. Here are some of their justifications:

A · VIEW · OF
LONDON
HIGHBURY FIELDS
CAMDEN PASSAGE
HYDE PARK
SOTHEBY'S
CHRISTIE'S
SOMERSET HOUSE
BUCKINGHAM PALACE
SOUTH KENSINGTON
FLATS FOR SALE
EARL'S COURT
BATTERSEA
STOCKWELL
N
W
E
S
FLATS TO LET
CLAPHAM
WANDSWORTH COMMON
STREATHAM

'It's only ten minutes from the City.'
'The gardens are so much bigger here.'
'It takes even less time to get to the West End than from Holland Park.'
'And of course it is much more convenient to get to the country.'
'Dailies are so easy to find locally.'
'It's so villagey.'
'It's so easy to walk the dog.'
'The tennis courts in Battersea are much better than over the river.'

Today's NPs will migrate deep into the SWs and Ws but they are uneasy about transposing their gentrification skills on the Ns and NWs where inverted snobbery runs rampant. Anyway, they can't afford St John's Wood, Hampstead, Highgate and Regent's Park. And in trendy counter-cultural boroughs like Islington, their plummy accents are all too often met with hostility. NPs don't experience this so much in 'sarf' London where the natives regard their new-found noble neighbours with a mixture of bemusement and indifference.

But there are some isolated pockets of NPs in parts of Islington like Ripplevale Grove, Highbury Fields and around Camden Passage. Like the British in Borneo, NPs residing in this aggressive *Guardian*-reading country react by retrenching into tribal mores and make a point of 'doing the right thing'. In order to distinguish themselves from the pot-smoking, sandal-shod rabble in the dwellings around them, such NPs become compulsive about arcane social niceties like sliding the Safeways port the right way round the table.

TENEMENT OF YOUTH

The compromise of NPs who have moved flats from Belgravia to Fulham is nothing to the insecurity and occasional squalor experienced by nomadic young NPs who shift from basement to attic all over London waiting till their family trust in its wisdom deems it appropriate to splutter up a capital sum as a down payment for a small property.

There are few rooms which now rent for under £30 per week (exclusive of other outgoings); and the state of the accommodation varies from functional at best to tacky at worst. Many NP girls are prepared to share a bedroom to save a sorely needed £15 a week: 'It plays hell with your love life, but I'd either have to get a job in the evening as well or move to cheaper accommodation in somewhere like Streatham,' says one NP girl.

Many NPs find the most depressing aspect of flatsharing is always being at the whim of some truculent landlord or landlady who holds the lease. 'Unless you are prepared to fit in totally with them the entire time or let yourself be sufficiently dominated to give them the confidence, the longest you can last in a flatshare is six months,' says one footsore NP who has trodden the flatshare beat round London.

For these NPs, making regular weekend visits to the country is of paramount importance, whatever the cost of the petrol or the train fare. It is not that their families provide them with free food, free drink and laundry facilities. It is that their family home and their family's position in the country is the only aspect of their lives that gives them their cultural identity. 'If I couldn't go back home at least every other weekend, I think I'd go mad,' says one not untypical NP. 'I mean, there'd be nothing to distinguish me otherwise from just another inconsequential urban pauper.'

In socialist boroughs the ruling reds, up from under the beds, speak indignantly of residents like Lady Olga Maitland as 'the blues between the blankets'.

The paucity of affordable, attractive property in London has meant that it is not uncommon for NPs in their mid-twenties still to live at home. Clinging to the parental jodhpur straps, these NPs are reluctant to leave a world where Floris bath oil, Twining's Earl Grey tea and Gordon's gin are generously supplied despite severe financial deprivation. Better a comfortable nest, they feel, than a few scrappy twigs. 'I am prepared to live with my parents [in Chelsea] so I can carry on enjoying myself,' says Karen Humphries, an attractive ex-debutante in her mid-twenties . . . 'rather that than sharing a terraced house in Clapham and struggling to pay the bills'.

To live at the right address, some London NPs are prepared to put up with an absence of furnishings. Karen Humphries, at one point, was living in a house with no kitchen, two chairs and only one bed for six months. She stresses that this isn't rare: 'There's a girl round the corner called Catherine Donville who inherited her house from an aunt. For a long time she couldn't afford to furnish it. Whenever she gave a dinner party she'd have to haul her aunt's old garden furniture into the grand dining-room.'

The town NP most envied by his peers is the one who has managed to hang on to a floor of his family town house in the form of a self-contained flat. Here, surrounded by fading family heirlooms, this NP often spends his days warding off creditors who insist upon squabbling with him over such paltry matters as heating bills. The NP fortunate enough to have held on to his former lifestyle would rather suffer a case of hypothermia than relinquish these memories of glorious things past.

NP's who live south of the river are now often referred to as Soanlies — " *'S only* five minutes from Sloane Square."

THE HOME

On buying his town residence the NP all too often finds that he has spent so much on procuring a good address or large garden that he has got hardly anything left over for decoration or conversion. This would not matter too much if young NPs didn't have such a strong predilection for acquiring old, if not derelict, edifices possessing what they term as 'potential'. Invariably the result for the first couple of years is that the NP home's decorative state is not far removed from 'haute' collapse as he laboriously reconstructs a kitchen and bathroom and repositions a wall which, one day, will enclose a drawing-room.

As most NPs can afford to do up only one room every six months, a strain can sometimes develop with the wife or live-in girlfriend who, understandably, is not too wild about sharing her home with a concrete mixer. The NP man finds that his most tolerant cohabiter is an NP woman, who, as one of a resilient breed, prides herself on her toughness in the face of acute discomfort. She chooses not to notice the splattered paint on her Midas shoes, nor the sawdust clinging to the hem of her Belville Sassoon taffeta gown. In the last century, Lady Burton, wife and travelling companion of Nile explorer Sir Richard, spoke the thoughts of many an NP woman today when, in the malarial lower delta, she declared: 'I can't think how a parvenue woman would cope if she had to put up with the things that I do.'

HOW NPs FURNISH THEIR FLATS

Upon setting up his first flat the young NP usually gets a few odds and ends from the division of spoils of the family estate. If no bequests are forthcoming, Mother is usually good about 'lending' a few essential items like vases, lamps and perhaps a moth-eaten bed-spread from the attic. His old tuck box is good for propping up the television, as well as indicating his public-school pedigree. It is likely he will inherit some pieces of cumbersome Edwardian furniture from a great-aunt in Inverness. Attaching some spurious sentimental affection to these 'family' belongings, he will have them transported down to his Wandsworth flat at a cost far exceeding their value. It never occurs to him that he could make a substantial saving by selling the effects at a local highland auction and use the proceeds to place his own bids closer to home.

He then relies on cast-offs from other members of the esoteric NP community who, unlike the ancien riche, are sympathetic to the difficulties of their own tribe. Among NPs, blood is at least as thick as claret. He can usually pick up a lopsided wingback chair or a beat-up old chesterfield this way.

For those few minor items his donors neglected to provide, like beds and tables, he patronizes downmarket auctions where he instinctively recognizes pieces with the best provenance, i.e. sold by other NPs. He probably also purchases a few rickety old frames, some dust-infested carpets and painted pine chests to which he applies a little imagination and even more elbow grease to transform them into items worthy to grace his Stockwell drawing-room.

As a last resort NPs will consort with antique dealers. This is the only time the NP admits to being 'in trade'. This painful degradation of his station saves the NP a sorely needed fifteen per cent. The NP's favourite antique shop is Heirloom & Howard (Armorial Antiques, 1 Hay Hill, London W1, 01 493 5868) where the proprietors keep an eye open for goods that once belonged to his family. One newly married NP couple were recently informed that the shop had for sale six dining chairs with the NP's family crest beautifully inlaid on the splats. At £7,000 the chairs sadly went to a richer buyer, yet the NP couple still hang on to the Polaroids of the chairs and show *them* off instead. Well, it's *nearly* as good . . .

It is only tourists who go out to the country, meander down obscure lanes, spot a weathered signpost with ANTIQUES in large letters and believe they've stumbled upon a 'find'. NPs know that antiques are generally cheaper in London than in the country.

ONLY HIS ART DEALER KNOWS FOR SURE

The bumbling aristocrat misguidedly transforming a pair of Ming vases into table lamps, carpeting the bathroom with a Caucasian Shirvan rug (making carefully sure to cut out a space to fit the loo) and laying an axe to the refectory table for firewood is about as accurate a representation as the working-class Andy Capp keeping coal in the bath and pigeons in the loft.

In these trying times, aristocrats who are careless about their belongings exist only in humorous fiction. NPs are only too aware of the price their possessions might fetch and know the exact market value of every item they own, from the silver tea strainer to the ivory-handled hairbrush. Calculating NPs cultivate relationships with art experts and are endlessly having them round to tea or over for the weekend to discuss what they could get for that Gainsborough portrait of the first Viscount or that croquet set he hasn't 'used in yonks'. Whatever the outlay for the hospitality, the NP thinks he has made a bargain: it saves him the one and a half per cent valuation fee.

NP AUCTION HOUSES

- ☞ *Bonhams' New Chelsea Galleries*
  65–69 Lots Road, London SW10
  01 352 0466
- ☞ *Lots Road Galleries*
  71 Lots Road, London SW10
  01 352 2349
- ☞ *Phillips West 2*
  10 Salem Road, London W2
  01 221 5303
- ☞ *Christie's (South Kensington)*
  85 Old Brompton Road, London SW7
  01 581 2231

When NPs have house sales fellow NPs are quick to attend the auctions where they hope to get the junk rejected by the dealers.

MOVING INTO THE NEW HOME

DECORATION: DEPLOYMENT, STRATEGY AND EFFECT

The brief most NPs give their decorators is: 'Renovate, don't innovate.' They believe in 'leaving well enough alone' and have grown fond of shabbiness and delapidation which illustrate, better than Debrett's, the ancient lineage from which they have sprung. NPs invariably prefer the bulging eyesores of antiquity to the straight lines of today's plasterers.

Where others might begin on their home by shielding themselves from nature with double-glazed windows, DIY damp-proofing and central heating, such considerations come low with NPs. When decorating their homes, most NPs unconsciously emulate the habitat of their childhood, i.e. a damp, cold, draughty but grand pile in the shires.

This usually means their priorities are the opposite of everyone else's. First they like to hang the chandelier inherited from Uncle Wilfred. Then they will lovingly restore the boarded-up fireplace. The right material for the curtains will be lengthily debated along with the overall colour scheme. Only after all this will the NP consider fixing the broken roof tiles, exchanging the rusting fuse box and replacing the cracked bathroom sink.

The most vexing problem for the NP is his drawing-room. It is, after all, his social stage. Is it any wonder then that he requisitions the best props he can lay his noble hands upon? Here, the NP's most illustrious furniture will be deployed – a Chippendale desk, a Regency card table and perhaps a Robert Adam cabinet (first-generation NPs always manage to hang on to at least two valuable antiques). Then there will be furnishings of similar vintage, though of lesser quality and more stricken condition. First-time guests often have trouble in comfortably reposing on the NP's sagging sofa, those chairs with the broken splats and the stool with the splintered legs.

Not that the NP fails to appreciate the new or the refurbished. The reason he retains his 150-year-old tattered lampshades is not because he is holding out for the highest bid from the local museum, but because to replace them with new silk equivalents would cost upwards of £300. Instead of settling for 'ghastly pseudo-silk', he simply pretends not to notice that they are in ribbons.

If the NP is particularly broke he might well supplement his sparse inherited furnishings with, for instance, a tea chest, camouflaged with an old linen cloth. But unless it matched his view of good taste, he'd not dream of sullying the drawing-room with modern furnishings. Cut-price bargains at furniture stores like MFI tempt the NP not a jot. He would pay *not* to have an immaculate three-piece Dralon suite. The ideal NP chaise longue is a dog-bitten chesterfield with protruberant horsehair stuffing (indicates long family use).

If the NP has a surplus of furniture, rather than suffer the sentimental anguish of selling it, hefty cabinets and chunky wardrobes will be heaved into unorthodox habitats like the kitchen and bathroom. Many a peer, moving abode, hangs landscapes above the Aga and lines bathroom walls with mahogany shelves.

NPs will happily compromise in their choice of televisions and hi-fi systems. Where the self-respecting middle-class executive's

lounge won't be without a twenty-eight-inch television, VHS video, Dolby cassette player, an Atari home computer and the other status symbols of domestic technology, the NP will be more than happy with a second-hand black and white television and, when he can get it to work, a Grundig valve radio-gramophone. Hardware for the NP still means a particularly tough pair of Lobb's shoes so it is unlikely he will feel the need for a home computer. Anyway, he is at pains to see the place in his domain for some costly gadget which cannot even be programmed to serve a simple gin and tonic. The strides of the electronic era make no impression on the NP.

Neither do the seductive blandishments of carpet manufacturers. The NP would seldom invest in wall to wall carpeting. If, however, a well-woven Wilton is already down, he might save himself the effort of removing it and simply scatter over it some old rugs. Otherwise he will sand down the floorboards, polish them, varnish them or perhaps even paint them.

Though the NP has come to terms with central heating elsewhere in the house, he prefers heaving shovelfuls of coal into the drawing-room grate. It might be messy, time-consuming and even uneconomic but it is an atavistic habit the traditional NP finds difficult to break. He won't even compromise by installing a gas log fire. He won't wear synthetic fibres, so how can he allow his chimney to exude fake fumes?

Fortunately, contemporary fashions provide the NP with dignity as well as ersatz substitutes for the grandeur of yesteryear. He may no longer be able to afford a gardener, but it doesn't take green fingers to nurture potted plants. Reconstructing a Georgian fireplace may be out of his stunted financial reach, but he can always take (and often does) Jocasta Innes's *Paint Magic* out of the library and study techniques of marbling for an otherwise innocuous mantelpiece or learn to rag roll (which is to a cracked wall what foundation is to a wrinkled face). The NP might be depressed by not being able to afford French silk curtains, but if it is not beyond the powers of his bank balance, for £10.95 Diana Phipps can teach him a trick or two in her decorating bible *Affordable Splendour*.

Nor does the NP shirk from soiling his aristocratic fingers and noble brow with the toil and sweat of manual labour. Building is in his blood. Didn't his ancestors spend hours drafting designs of follies to enliven their demesnes? And didn't they stroll about supervising their men in the construction of the fruits of their imagination: picturesque grottoes, palatial pagodas and cascading waterfalls?

Why then, with the accoutrements of DIY, he should find it as easy as the foxtrot to brandish saw, drill and paintbrush in the task of converting his Fulham house. Undeterred by mundane considerations like inexperience, the NP attempts the feats of joining bookshelves, plastering walls and attaching moulding. With subtle shades of Bollom paint he will fastidiously sponge his walls.

These projects meet with varying degrees of success. More often than not however, the NP bungles the job, scraps the whole idea and resorts to calling in a professional to put things right, especially in the sophisticated area of broken paint finishes like stippling. But here the NP confronts a further anxiety: should he employ one of the scores of his own kind who have set up shop in this field or should he hire the services of a fifth-generation specialist? He feels a class loyalty to his fellow NPs yet the East End origins of the others instil him with the confidence that they can actually finish the job. Often, though, the exorbitant quotes of the latter put him off. East Enders *still* think a posh accent translates into a bottomless bank balance.

Unsurprisingly NPs have a particular penchant for trompe l'oeil which can lend grandeur to the meanest house in Wandsworth. So many murals now adorn these artisans' abodes, it seems a Renaissance revival is under way. Trompe l'oeil painters are the Mantegnas of the eighties; NPs, though on a diminutive financial scale, are the latterday Gonzagas.

The NP demand to create delusions of splendour out of the hard reality of plasterboard has given rise to a new industry. Even solicitors and other professionals have abandoned secure jobs in the City for the more lucrative employment of catering to the NP's grandiose whims. Classical landscapes, romantic grottoes, fake cornices and dadorails are only some of the motifs these artists conjure up in order to revive the NP's sentimental yearning for past domestic glory.

Decorating Courses

A long time has passed since the upper classes could rely upon good, cheap labour in the upkeep of their home. To Her Ladyship's dismay, she has discovered that walls don't paint themselves. To her credit she has often taken the back-breaking job upon herself. Where she once wouldn't have been able to identify a paintbrush, she has now become an expert on when to employ a silk vinyl or a matt finish. NP wives flock to expensive decorating courses to learn stippling, dragging, rolling and the like. NP woman is convinced that the initial expenditure will be more than made up in the years of saving decorators' fees.

See Artisan Courses ('Education')

Despite his resourceful abilities there remain, however, some blindspots in the NP's overall decorative and refurbishing masterplan, namely the kitchen and bathroom. However primeval their condition his interest in improving their amenities and aesthetic state is in inverse proportion to his efforts elsewhere. Only a tough wife will get her NP husband to invest in these rooms he grumpily dismisses as 'merely functional'. She even has to fight to get rid of the pitted metal loo-paper box they inherited from the last owner. 'But darling, why waste our money on some absurd porcelain roller?' he'll ask wonderingly.

Visitors say the most striking aspects of the prototypical NP decor are the huge gilt frames housing mildewed mirrors and life-sized portraits of gout-ridden baronets. Designed for the proportions of the NP's ancestral Scottish castle, their effect is to make his four-roomed maisonette off the Wandsworth Bridge Road more diminutive than it already is.

NPs without a gallery of family oils are not too proud to hang reproductions. The NP rule is that they must be favourite *lesser* works of art, for instance, a menu designed by Cocteau. Popular works are *too* blatant. A famous post-impressionist poster that could be found in any Crouch End semi would never disgrace the walls of an NP. This rule also applies to prints. The more remote and esoteric the artist, the better.

In among the framed family snaps on the drawing-room table or mantelpiece, older NPs especially have at least one fading sepia photograph of a wing of the ancestral mansion before it was blown up, relinquished to the National Trust or flogged to pay off death duties. An impressive line-up of servants will be noted alongside a coach-sized limousine. When some unexpected bill darkens his noble threshold the NP often gazes upon this vision of a carefree and plutocratic past and in melancholic moments asks himself where it all went wrong.

SERVANTS

According to Mrs Isabella Beeton, in 1906 a household with the scant income of £1,000 a year (£25,000 today after tax) could employ a cook, housemaid and perhaps a manservant. A grand household like Longleat employed no fewer than forty-three servants from chef to lamp boy and including six laundry maids and two sewing maids. The outdoor servants nearly doubled the number. But now NPs, like the colonials who returned from the British Raj, have had to readjust from the privileges of a king to the duties of a kitchen boy.

Less destitute NPs still employ a daily who usually comes in weekly. NPs wives feel comfortable with their status as mistress and don't feel the middle-class compunction to scurry round the house tidying up before the daily arrives. If anything, she may overwork her charge as she is still unable to differentiate between the duties of a daily and those of scullery maid, nursery maid and upstairs maid. But her charming and authoritarian manner (See Common Touch) enable her to maintain the services of a domestic on a lackey basis with no complaints.

There are many NPs who can no longer afford to have any servants at all. As in all other aspects of their life, NPs have faced this upset with stoic composure. The NP man is especially jolly about performing household chores and has even grown to enjoy hoovering, cooking and emptying dustbins. He will help his wife with most things, but draws the line at scrubbing his own floors. They just fade from his selective vision.

Here are some of the excuses NPs use for not employing servants. As usual, lack of money is never one of them.

'I just couldn't bear to have anyone living in the house.'

'You can't get good help these days.'

'I found it just too *boring having to listen to their personal problems.'*

'None of them can speak English these days.'

■

GARDENS

The gardens of Fulham NPs are usually no larger than a grand piano. The NP is fond of referring to this concrete enclosure as 'parkland'. The pathetic confine is brilliantly decked out with assorted objects found in rubbish tips. Water cisterns support herb beds and bricks support flower pots in these thin versions of Arcadia. One Fulham NP gardener proudly proclaims: 'I have a robin and two bees in my garden. One learns to count these things.'

ALLOTMENTS

Some NPs who have lost their ancestral acres and rolling lawns have been careful not to forfeit any claim to be labelled 'landed' – even when their portion of England's green and pleasant land happens to be a 6′ × 18′ allotment off a North London railway siding.

Throughout spring and summer evenings the NP's atavistic knowledge of the earth can be put to profitable use cultivating a harvest of carrots, parsley, cabbages and leeks. However, last year an NP who engaged in this chic pastime for Londoners was dismayed to read an alarming report that vegetables grown in the Greater London area cannot be consumed now without fear of also devouring a dangerously high percentage of contaminous lead. But not believing in needless waste, the NP magnanimously presented the season's crop to his mother-in-law.

FLOWERS

Profuse arrangements of cut flowers and other decorous foliage are not only essential for stating the NP's Arcadian roots, but they are also handy for camouflaging that crack in the wall or distracting the eye from that mildewed bureau.

Flowers are particularly important at the

dinner parties of NPs who have long ago sold their silverware and candelabra. The worse the condition of the vase, the more abundant the arrangement.

Every NP household has got a garden . . . or access to one. Young NPs raid their parents' flowerbeds on weekend visits. They also know the best evenings to sneak into the alleyway behind Sloane Street and select flowers discarded from the Pulbrook & Gould tip. One NP from Cheyne Walk was stopped by the police as she picked cow parsley on the hard shoulder of the M4. She managed, however, to get away with a large bouquet which was soon gracing her drawing-room's grand piano.

NPs, of course, know every trick there is for prolonging the lifespan of their fresh flora, whether peony or weed. One grand NP hostess uses a clever ploy discovered inadvertently by one of her guests. This hostess always displays a magnificent flower arrangement in the drawing-room of her stately home. One day a guest, finding herself alone, took the opportunity to sniff the bouquet. She was somewhat taken aback to discover that mixed in with the common garden flowers were two dozen silk roses. No wonder she had always been impressed by the floral abundance.

Making silk flowers is also an NP activity. NP Clare Davison sells hers at Nimmo's, Elystan Street, London SW5. Telephone number: 01 584 1008 (appt. only). It goes without saying that if an NP is going to fake something, she does it in style. Nothing less than silk imitation flowers would be even remotely acceptable to NPs.

NPs feel that as long as the arrangement is dramatic, its contents make little difference. One NP decorates her refectory table with tall sprigs of rosemary buried in a slender silver vase.

■

THE COUNTRY HOUSE

The great houses remain, but only half
are inhabited
Dusty the gun rooms and the stable
clocks stationary

▪

W.H. AUDEN, 1936

No one should be fooled by a grand address in the country. Many NPs occupy impressive-sounding manor houses, halls and castles, but few get to experience the many joys of living in an historical landmark.

Inheriting the ancestral home is often more a curse than a godsend. When a New Zealand farmer recently became the Earl of Mount Edgcumbe, he inherited nearly a million pounds of capital transfer taxes along with his Cornish estate. Maintenance and upkeep alone will cost His Lordship the same again if he lives there for life. The sensible business-minded person would sell up. Yet NPs are as attached to their ancestral homes as seaweed is to rock. It takes a rough storm to wrench them out.

For many the climate *has* been rough. Because of the expense of upkeep, nearly 2,000 great country houses have been abandoned since 1870. In these taxing NP days, when an NP inherits his estate he will probably find himself in the same position as the peer who was told upon receiving his inheritance: 'You're a millionaire on paper, but you can't afford a bicycle.'

NPs abound particularly in Scotland where houses are ludicrously cheap compared to similar accommodation in England, though running them is as expensive. One London NP with a flat in Fulham was idly considering buying a castle in the Highlands, though solely for the prestige. The price? £5,000.

THE ESTATE

The poor man in his castle
The rich man at his gate
Taxation's hit the landed
And disordered their estate

Even the most financially stretched of the landed classes cannot technically be called 'poor'. For today anyone with more than 500 English acres is worth at least half a million pounds. But the fact is, capital-rich does not mean cash-rich. The farmer with a thousand well-managed acres may generate enough cash to put in stocks and bonds; but the NP with a sizeable country mansion has to plough the fruits of his acres into the upkeep of his home.

Lord Jermyn, son and heir of the Marquis of Bristol, maintains that even families who hold tens of thousands of acres are already to some extent NPs: 'The Britain-based aristocracy live like complete paupers,' says the multi-millionaire. 'They're land-heavy. They have no spending power and in the end they go broke,' he adds.

The usual pattern of decline starts with the debt-ridden NP selling off a few fields. But without sufficient acres to support the outgoings of his house, his home soon goes too. If capital taxes increase, today's landed lords may be tomorrow's bedsit barons.

When death duties were the principal capital tax, a prosperous peer could avoid making his heir an NP if he followed a set path prescribed by a proficient accountant through the maze of legislation loopholes. Now, with the introduction of Capital Transfer Tax, the loopholes have virtually vanished. NPs gaze wistfully to their compatriots on the continent, most of whom are taxed on what they spend, rather than what they own. The landed NP who scrimps and saves even on his groceries ruefully contemplates that were he in that happy position, he would hardly be taxed at all.

In the meantime four options lie open to the landed: they become tax exiles; they sell up; they battle on taking the best (or more often worst) advice available; they give up and hand their property over to the National Trust (if they will take it).

TAX EXILE

Till recently Earl Jermyn's solution was to hire platoons of lawyers and accountants, create a web of offshore companies and live abroad nine months of the year. While other nobles lock horns with the Inland Revenue to hang on to their estates, Jermyn, in the last seven years, has tripled his not insubstantial fortune. Certainly most of the measures he initiated were a revolutionary departure. For instance, Ickworth, his ancestral estate, was controlled from an office in Paris.*

But moving abroad is regarded by most aristocrats as bad form and a financial last resort. It's much more unpatriotic than fiddling taxes. Furthermore, to reap the benefits, most landed families would have to sell up completely, the dimmest prospect imaginable.

* Jermyn returned to Britain earlier this year when Chancellor Nigel Lawson reduced Capital Transfer Tax. But experts agree that when the Conservatives are voted out of power, this concession to the 'landed' will be revoked and the likes of Lord Jermyn will abandon Britain once more.

SELLING UP

A mother would be more willingly separated from her baby than most aristocrats from their estates. The investment analyst might simply regard a thousand acres of farmland as a useful part of a portfolio, one day to be disposed of at a good market price. But to the landed family, their ancestral acres are an integral feature of their identity, roots, status and character.

Nor is it even that easy for the family to sell up. For a long time palatial mansions have attracted virtually no buyers, except the occasional rich foreigner (for the most part Arab or American) or fringe religious sect. Between the wars, the impoverished squire of Kirtlington park, Gloucestershire, sold his acres to a hunting family whose own land had been encroached upon by housing estates. Having negotiated a good price for the acres, the squire broached the sensitive topic of the uneconomic mansion. 'And as regards the house, I shall require . . .' he said, 'a good box of cigars'!

The NP wishing to sell up also has to face the powerful conservationist lobby which feels the NP's heritage is also the nation's – perhaps even more so.

When the tax-hit peer, Lord Brownlow, put his estate, his mansion and all its treasures on the market, he was berated by moralizing diatribes in the national press. The next time a debt-pressed peer has to sell off even a painting, observe the vilification he endures if the highest price is from a foreigner and the work has to go abroad.

Others who have sold off most of their land might well have a manor house with galleries of Old Masters. 'Why not flog that Dutch seascape?' a helpful acquaintance might suggest. 'A similar work went for £50,000 at Christie's last month.' Alas for most NPs. They are only trustees of their family treasures, i.e. the Reynolds, the Stubbs and the Gainsborough are in reality owned by the Inland Revenue. This deal with the treasury works as follows: the NP family is allowed to hold on to the family treasures, but as soon as they try and sell them they have to pay a backlog of capital taxes. The Stubbs might well go for half a million in the sale room, but its revenue to the NP will hardly pay the rates, let alone mend the two acres of leaking roof.

BATTLING ON

Most NPs opt to remain in their crumbling, draughty, ancestral homes, tilling the land like bucolic squires of yesteryear. But because of taxation, few estates can remain agriculturally viable far into the future. An estate making a reasonable profit can dive into loss when its acres are eroded by a huge capital transfer tax levy with the passing of every generation. Punitive taxes call for imaginative countermeasures. So many an ancestral holding is now subsidized by activities not wholly in keeping with the rural Eden envisioned by its creators.

To save his home from physical collapse and himself from financial, the NP is prepared to blow up a wing or to move the family living quarters to a single floor where he can mull over ambitious business schemes no matter how unedifying, vulgar or improbable. Thirty years ago when the Duke of Bedford converted part of his grounds into a safari park to draw large crowds to Woburn Abbey, a voluble caucus of peers protested that he was letting the side down with such a commercial gimmick. This tribal snobbery has proved too dear for the upper classes. Today there are few peers with stately homes who are wealthy enough to live in them as they were originally intended. Squires by the scores have, through necessity, now evolved into ringmasters, their homes into money-generating circuses: paddocks are transformed into funfairs; woods into adventure playgrounds; stables into boutiques; outhouses into emporiums for cottage-industry textiles – all in the drive for solvency.

Still laughing — The Earl of Suffolk and Berkshire who shares his ancestral seat with seventeen other families. *PHOTO: DAFYDD JONES*

The Duke of Marlborough not only manufactures glass paperweights in Blenheim Palace but lets out his grounds as a stage for pop stars like Barry Manilow. The magnificent Loseley House is now less famous as a stately home than as a top-quality dairy producing excellent yoghurt and ice cream. Viscount Chewton has now become a byword for his estate-produced cheese. His Lordship exports fifty-two tons of Chewton cheddar every year to Saudi Arabia.

Another trend among the aristocracy is to forfeit privacy by subdividing ancestral homes into blocks of flats. If a house is propitiously built, only the wings need be sold or rented off, leaving the centre section for the family. Many NPs find the notion of sharing their home, like the Earl of Suffolk, with seventeen other families, somewhat alarming. Yet it does mean they can actually afford to reside in their hereditary seat – or at least a few rooms in it.

If his house is spectacular the NP can also make money by renting it out to film and television companies. Michael Saunders Watson leased Rockingham Castle to the Earl of Pembroke, the producer of the Civil War series 'By the Sword Divided'. In a letter to the Historic Housing Association Mr Saunders Watson reported that though he enjoyed his contribution to television drama it did have one drawback: 'It is difficult,' he wrote, 'to concentrate in one's office as riderless horses, dripping in blood, come charging through the towers into the forecourt and Roundheads come pouring over the wall.'

A more traditional method for NPs hoping to refill their coffers is to apply for planning permission for remote borders of their estates. It is these NPs who will put off creditors, telling them, 'Some frightful property spiv is talking to the estate about putting up Barratt's houses.' This is possible in the home counties, but the aspiring NP developer is being more optimistic than practical if his acres happen to be situated in some bogland on the fens or some far-flung Scottish moor.

Among the shakey stately home enterprises there are some unexpected success stories. When he was a young man, the Marquess of Hertford was advised that Ragley Hall, his ancestral seat, was uneconomic and he should have to sell up. But by applying strict business principles, the Marquess succeeded in making the house and the estate profitable. Like many owners seeking to optimize financially on their ancestral seats, the Marquess turned his stately home into a stately guest house. Bed and breakfast at His Lordship's is just over £100.

The Marquess of Hertford, however, had difficulty making his mother, the resident dowager, understand some of the implemented economies. When he explained to her that the cost of keeping a couple of cows merely to produce the household's butter was more expensive, pound for pound, than caviar, the bewildered Marchioness replied: 'But darling, I don't like caviar!'

Another peer whose finances are assisted by foreign paying guests is the Earl of Normanton. His sixteen-bedroomed mansion, Somerley in Hampshire, is on the books of two agents. Having successfully applied for a drinks licence, His Lordship has cheerfully put himself in charge of serving to save the cost of staff. 'I'm afraid it's all very necessary to keep the house going – every little bit helps,' says Lady Normanton. 'We shall do whatever people's needs require,' she humbly adds.

OPENING TO THE PUBLIC

Many a landed NP's most precious asset is to be found right under his very patrician nose. His house, grounds, outbuildings and personal items all jointly contribute to the museum value in showing the public how the other half per cent used to live.

The NP's new-found relationship with the masses is a symbiotic one: he needs their entrance fees; they seek vicarious grandeur. Times may not be what they were, but so long as the public appear in sufficient numbers and the profits cover the running costs, his deal is not necessarily a bad one. The problem for NPs is that the number of country-house visitors has fallen at the same rate his maintenance costs have risen!

THE REALITY The NP who opens his house to the public is usually in for some rude shocks. Life does not suddenly become a bed of Tudor roses just because he makes the sacrifice of allowing tens of thousands of coughing, shouting and spitting tourists through his portals. And just because he has painstakingly listed opening hours in official brochures does not preclude visits from unexpected guests at unlisted times. The owner of Brympton d'Evercy in Somerset was gardening in his underpants when his first visitors drew up in a coach.

'Within minutes of their arrival they were crawling like ants over an old apple core, upstairs, downstairs, cellars, attics. Fast as I hurried them out of one door,' says Charles Clive-Ponsonby-Fane 'they trotted round to another side entrance, up another back staircase, poking into doors, cupboards, passages and pantries.'

The Earl and Countess of Cawdor now move to a house in the woods every summer to avoid the perusing hordes. 'Every time you looked out of the window there was a child not of your loins pulling up the roses,' remarked the indignant Earl.

INSURANCE Others have more than roses lifted. Guarding against burglary is difficult for the NP. Nor can he afford to insure against the nimble-fingered thief walking off with the odd Fabergé egg or Ming vase. Even the comparatively wealthy Marquess of Bath cannot afford to insure the contents of Longleat. At a one and a quarter per cent premium, he would have to pay at least £100,000 a year for the possessions valued in excess of £8 million.

PROFITS Most NPs who open their home soon discover to their dismay that incomings rarely match outgoings. They will be lucky if the entrance fees cover basic costs like food, never mind luxuries like repairing the cupola, restoring the Van Dyke or reupholstering the sofa.

The owners of smaller houses who open them are happy if they can cover even a third to a half their maintenance costs with the proceeds, though most never achieve anywhere near this according to the Historic Houses Association. It seems that for every penny that is taken in from the relentless stream of visitors, another goes out to pay the Port-a-Loo people, the Wall's ice-cream man or the butcher who supplies carcases for the lions.

The Marquess of Tavistock says that even the famous Woburn Abbey is a bad business investment. Despite tempting tens of thousands of daytrippers to the Abbey with their dolphinarium, forty-two antiques shops, Roux brothers' restaurant and myriad other attractions, Woburn lost £230,000 in one recent financial year.

USAGE & ABUSAGE Extraordinarily enough, the room names in stately homes

Full Repairing Leases

NP estates are inconveniently cluttered with a spate of outbuildings such as hunting lodges and cottages that are rampant with rodents and dissolving in damp. No self-respecting farm labourer would be seen dead in these dilapidated ruins. The remedy lies in the NP granting full repairing leases on a peppercorn rent to fellow NPs. So delighted are these town NPs to have a 'country place' of their own for a mere £15 per week, that they fail to register the small print which decrees that they have to renovate the building totally before returning it to the owner twenty or so years hence.

once corresponded to their actual uses. Reading took place in libraries; dancing in ballrooms. But once the NP opens his home, the only books read in the library are guide books and the only movement that takes place in the NP's ballroom is the jitterbug shuffle of filing tourists. Though even today the State Rooms are kept at the ready for a possible royal visit, it is more than likely the only HRHs whose presence will grace these chambers is Hundreds of Roaming Hordes.

VOYEURISM The down side of opening to the public is of course lack of privacy. But it is consoling for NPs to learn that there is also a positive aspect. NPs need not worry when their Sunday tea runs slightly over schedule and there is no time to brush away the scone crumbs, nor air out the lagging smell of Earl Grey and toast before the snuffling, inquisitive herd is let through the rope barrier. It gives the house that 'lived in' feel so important towards establishing credibility with the marginally incredulous crowds. The NP family mansion may appear a trifle ramshackle compared to its former glory, yet the multitude of uninitiated commoners will otherwise be sceptical that the place is in fact a single family dwelling. Tourists like nothing better than to slyly observe the present while, under the guise of antiquarian interest, pretend to peruse relics of the past. Seeing the family go about their mundane daily business gives the visitors a sense of authenticity rather like a zoo where animals are allowed to roam free in their natural habitat.

LOSING THE BATTLE

Each year there are more reports of owners giving up the struggle. To pass on Ugbrooke, his ancestral seat, to his son, Lord Clifford of Chudleigh has had to decamp to a three-bedroomed cottage in Guernsey. His financial advisers had warned him that death duties would otherwise ruin his family and break up the estate. 'I am heartbroken at the thought of leaving, but it is the only solution,' said Lord Clifford, who felt his enforced exile to be 'poor reward for hard work' in restoring the house. In a letter explaining his move to his thirteen tenants, he said: 'The last thing on earth I want to do is to move from the place I consider I have saved. Financially I shall be much worse off, so no snide remarks about a tax haven please.'

Ancestrally homeless NPs tend to move to a nearby rectory, estate lodge or dower house when they don't move to the Channel Islands.

In the country traditions die hard and a distinguished family name can continue to give an NP clout in the community long after the family have lost the wherewithal to back it. In the popular television series 'To the Manor Born', actress Penelope Keith depicted a country NP still commanding undiminished awe among the locals despite her landholding having been diminished to a gateway lodge. For this same reason NPs prefer not to move to the materially meritocratic suburbs which snobbish NPs refer to as 'life-peer land'.

The Earl and Countess of Devon recently had to move into a cottage because they couldn't afford the upkeep and outgoings of the sixty-eight-bedroomed Powderham Castle. Their family motto speaks for the thoughts of many an NP: 'Where have I fallen, what have I done?'

QUALIFICATION QUIZ

Before going through the rigours of opening his house to the madding crowd, the NP should not only weigh up his family's psychological aptitude for entering the leisure industry, but should also determine whether the public will deem his heritage sufficiently worthy of inspection. He must ask himself:

- **Are there more than thirty rooms in the house?**
- **Can I bear to turn the physic garden into a car park?**
- **Is there enough unchipped Wedgwood to warrant its display?**
- **Has a reigning monarch *ever* slept in the State Rooms?**
- **Was the house designed by either Vanburgh or Inigo Jones?**
- **Is that a real Titian above the fireplace? Or just a 'School of . . .'?**
- **Were any of the ancestral portraits painted by Van Dyke?**
- **Is the library ceiling really Adam?**
- **Was the garden landscaped by Capability Brown?**
- **Are the chairs Chippendale? Or early Maples . . .?**
- **Is at least one of the swags carved by Grinling Gibbons?**
- **Can the battlements hold the weight of coachloads of tourists?**
- **Can the dogs be relied upon not to bite strangers?**
- **Could the wife bear Port-a-Loos in the garden?**
- **Will she mind spending Sundays in the kitchen baking scones for the tea room?**
- **Will I mind being asked the same tiresome question about the beheading of the third Viscount?**
- **Will I mind impertinent strangers calling me cousin and insisting we share the same great grandmother?**

If the NP can answer satisfactorily to three-quarters of these questions, then he and his family are qualified in both legacy and temperament to open their home and be ogled for profit.

NATIONAL MISTRUST

The National Trust is not the featherbed for NPs that it used to be. Before the forties the terms for an NP donating his house to the Trust were often favourable to him. The Trust would sometimes:

* Take a property with no endowment.
* Guarantee that future generations had an absolute right to live in the house in perpetuity.
* Allow short visiting hours. (The Woolner family descendants of Pre-Raphaelite sculptor Stephen Woolner still have as part of their terms, the proviso that they need open their home, Bradley Manor in Devon, only one hour per week!)

But in today's taker's market, the givers are at a disadvantage. Nowadays the desperate NP who passes over his ancestral pile to the Trust, hands on his privacy and a huge chunk of his capital along with the rights of ownership.

Things have got to the point where:

* There are so many threatened properties and so few funds that even NPs with houses of indisputable national importance often have to beg the Trust to take theirs on.
* If the house is not self-supporting, the NP has to provide the Trust with an endowment in the form of either cash, land or investments in order to maintain its upkeep.
* The Trust will *not* guarantee that any future generations will continue as tenants.
* The NP is bound by strict terms concerning opening hours.
* The NP cannot add to any collection without the Trust's permission.
* The Trust occasionally takes furniture from the NP's home and displays it in another Trust property.

Charles Clive-Ponsonby-Fane, who owns the aforementioned Brympton d'Evercy in Somerset, has strong reservations about ever giving his house over to the National Trust. 'The Trust was set up to provide a safety net for our ancestral homes,' he says. 'But to get the National Trust to take your ancestral home, you have to endow it with enough money to maintain it, i.e. about a million pounds. If I had a million pounds, I wouldn't have to go to the Trust. But my chief objection is that there is no way of ever getting the property back once you have given it over. My grandson or daughter could make a million or two at the pools or dealing in African cocoa futures. But there is no way of getting the house back or even of getting a guarantee of becoming a tenant. I think the National Trust should provide such a facility.'

So does Premier Baronet of Great Britain, Sir Frances Dashwood, who lives with his family in West Wycombe, which his father handed over to the Trust. It grieves Sir Francis, that though he has made enough money in his lifetime, there is no legal way he can repossess the former family estate. He makes no bones about the inconveniences of living in a Trust property. He is not amused that three-quarters of the visitors are members of the Trust and thus pay no entrance fees. 'All they do is ruin the carpets and drive one away from the place,' he grumbles. He admits that he has deliberately situated tourist facilities like the garden centre and car park across the main road as a gesture towards protecting his family's precarious privacy by 'sucking people off from the house and keeping them happy'.

Sir Francis Dashwood: disenchanted with the *National Trust.* PHOTO: DAFYDD JONES

LISTED HOUSES

Often the Department of the Environment decides, without even letting the NP know, that his house is listed. This certainly lends status, but the NP can end up paying for this honour. It used to be that he could blow up a wing of his ancestral home if he couldn't manage the heating bills. Not so with a listed building.

Living in a listed building is like having one's cake but not being allowed to eat it. Technically the house still belongs to the NP, but he is restricted in what he can do with his own property. If his house is listed because of, say, its magnificent Palladian façade, the NP cannot even plant a hedge in the paddock without permission from the DoE.

Not only is the owner told what he can not do to his property, he is also told what he must. If he does not maintain it properly, the NP gets a Listed Building Repair Notice. This means that if he does not do the work then the local authority does it – and the NP gets the bill. If the NP cannot pay, the authority can then sell his house from under him. Listed house owners feel very wronged by their lack of rights.

NOT-SO-STATELY HOMES

It may seem that the larger the ancestral home, the greater the NP's hardship. But, in fact, the reverse is often true. Indeed, a British Tourist Authority survey has found that the smaller historical houses are the ones most threatened with extinction. This is not only because they are a bottom priority of the National Trust. Manor houses and smaller halls simply don't attract enough visitors to pay for opening costs. As lesser listed buildings, neither do they qualify for tax relief or grant aid.

MAINTENANCE & RUNNING COSTS

In the good old days, stately homes and the estate that encompassed them were the factories of the day, providing jobs for the local village folk who in turn supplied a cheap labour force. But this feudal mode of life has vanished. NP squires everywhere find themselves in the predicament of no longer being able to retile the roof, prune the topiary or dredge the ornamental pond at the mere utterance of a command. The NP landowner has had to learn to thumb through the yellow pages to locate firms of workers who specialize in these different areas of manual expertise. But after centuries of low wages, they have overcompensated by pricing themselves right out of the stately home owner's pocket. The result is that upper-class housing has begun to fall apart.

The cost of maintaining an historic house is three to four times more than that for a modern house of the same size. One of the largest differences is in flat roof repair. Where it costs about £10 a square yard for a modern home, it costs over £100 for an historic one.

Some NPs are lucky enough to qualify for the rare government grants to help with restoration. But, like a lot of NPs, David Fursdon, squire of Fursdon House in Devon, is unable to accept such a charitable offer because he is too poor to match the required balance of more than half from his own funds.

Many NPs don't realize how sensible it would be to demolish their Jacobean mansion and build a new one in its place. According to the Historic Houses Association, many country manses are in danger of irrevocable collapse often unbeknownst to the owners. Lord and Lady Methuen at least *knew* something had to be done to reinforce the upper floors of their ancestral home, Corsham Court. But like so many NPs, they put off the costly repairs too long. They regretted their procrastination, however, when two tons of masonry and plaster suddenly collapsed through the ceiling of the picture gallery.

NP mansions might have millions of bricks to repoint and miles of marble to polish, but even more costly, there are hundreds of thousands of cubic feet to heat and light. Though their forbears had been quite content with the negligible heating arrangements of their draughty halls, many of the post-war generation succumbed to the luxury of central heating. Fine for a bungalow, central heating is a nightmare in a palatial manor house. Aside from cracking the Constables and drying up the Davenport, heating constitutes one of the biggest drains on His Lordship's wealth. NPs trying to heat their houses economically cannot simply double-glaze their oriel windows nor instal insulation behind original oak panelling.

The heating and electricity of the Duke of Marlborough's seat, Blenheim Palace, runs to £50,000 a year, and His Grace lives in only one wing . . . and that for only a portion of the year. But with a turnover of £2 million a year, from the estate and visiting public, such outgoings can be accommodated.

Not so for Lord Snowdon's half-brother, the Earl of Rosse. On paper he might look rich, but he lives like an NP. Birr, his 100-roomed Irish castle, costs him £60 a day just for the central heating. Because his turnover from the visiting public and the yield from his estate is small, the Earl cannot afford to switch it on, so his family have to wear extra pullovers. Since he inherited the castle in 1981, he has had to sell off £300,000 of the castle's contents to pay off debts and keep it going. To get cheaper energy the Earl plans to run a turbine from his local river. Meanwhile his family will have to birrrr.

Restriction of lighting is, however, an unwise economy in most large country houses. There are just too many valuable items lying around. Why risk an unwary guest stumbling into a cabinet of Wemyss china in order to save the cost of a light-bulb?

Historic Houses Cost More to Maintain Because:

They are older and so need constant repairs from regilding mouldings to saving sinking foundations

They require special building materials: gesso is not mass-produced

They require rare craftwork skills: not every labourer knows how to treat *putti*

They need expensive architects: to supervise the workers over delicate repairs

NP COUNTRY HOUSE SURVIVAL KIT

HISTORIC HOUSES ASSOCIATION
38 Ebury Street, London SW1W 0LU
01 730 9419
It is for NPs what the AA is for motorists. It advises its members – owners of heritage properties – on the mechanics of maintaining and retaining their ancestral homes, from coping with taxes to plugging up leaky moats. As a succcessful parliamentary lobby group, it has been largely responsible for establishing the present safety net of protective heritage legislation.

NATIONAL TRUST
42 Queen Anne's Gate, London SW1H 9AS
01 222 9251
NPs who owe great fortunes to Her Majesty's Government often have no other option than to turn over their last remaining asset – their home, its contents and the land it rests upon – to the National Trust. The Inland Revenue taketh, and the NP giveth away. Yet only the owners of the grandest homes need bother to offer bequests. (See 'National Mistrust'.) After his donation, the NP and his family are allowed to stay in the house for at least the duration of the present generation and, it is hoped, more.

SOCIETY FOR THE PROTECTION OF ANCIENT BUILDINGS (SPAB)
37 Spital Square, London E1 6DY
01 377 1644
Advises on technical aspects of the preservation and conservation of old buildings from windmills to great country houses. 'No project is too small.' They believe in *protecting* a building, along with its architectural quirks, rather than *restoring* it with a capital 'R' and eliminating them. Publishes a useful newsletter for members, listing threatened buildings currently on the market.

VICTORIA & ALBERT MUSEUM
Cromwell Road, London SW7
01 589 6371
Their conservation workshops provide a wealth of information to NP house owners.

COUNTRY LANDOWNERS ASSOCIATION
16 Belgrave Square, London SW1X 8PQ
01 235 0511
Advises members on every aspect of land ownership from how to get a fair return on capital investment to how to obtain improved Capital Transfer Tax Relief. It champions NP causes by helping NPs to keep land in private hands and helps to fight 'planning blight'.

NATIONAL ASSOCIATION OF DECORATIVE AND FINE ARTS SOCIETIES (NADFAS)
38 Ebury Street, London SW1W 0LU
01 730 0341
Their Voluntary Conservation Corps supplies platoons of helpful ladies to aid NPs in scrubbing statues, cataloguing libraries, cleaning books and the like. Very good with polish. Along with members of the Women's Institute and the National Trust, they comprise the bulk of country-house visitors. Known by NPs affectionately as: National Association of Dragons and Fierce Aged Spinsters.

THE ASSOCIATION OF INCOMING TOUR OPERATORS
David Gerrard Travel
4 Odeon Parade, London NW10 8SA
Historic house and garden owners seeking to attract foreign visitors provide members of this association with leaflets giving details of cost and party booking arrangements.

NATIONAL TOURIST BOARDS: These are essentially free NP PR firms.

ENGLISH TOURIST BOARD
4 Grosvenor Gardens, London SW1W 0DU
01 730 3400

SCOTTISH TOURIST BOARD
23 Ravelston Terrace, Edinburgh EH4 3EU
031 332 2433

WALES TOURIST BOARD
2 Fitzalan Road, Cardiff CF2 1UY
0222 499909

All promote country houses within Great Britain.

BRITISH TOURIST AUTHORITY
64 St James's Street, London SW1W 1NF
01 629 9191
Promotes country houses abroad, hoping to attract overseas visitors.

CHRISTOPHER BUXTON
Period and Country Houses Ltd
61 Harcourt Terrace, London SW10
01 373 5180
Since he began in 1955, Christopher Buxton has restored and converted between forty-five and fifty great country houses including Charlton Park, the seat of the Earls of Suffolk and Berkshire for over 300 years. His usual *modus operandi* is to acquire a ninety-nine-year lease on a deteriorating ancestral home that the owners have virtually given up hope on. He then replans the house for multiple occupation. Having completed the apartments, he leases them out making sure first to set up a well-structured tenants' management committee. Because he is careful to spell out terms in advance, there have been no known problems of dissatisfied tenants so far.

KIT MARTIN
Save Britain's Heritage
68 Battersea High Street, London SW11
01 228 3336
Like Buxton, he crusades to save houses which would probably disappear without his intervention. His method is similar to Buxton's, except that he usually buys the freehold of the property. Among the conversions made by this architect is Hazells Hall, Bedfordshire, Francis Pym's ancestral home.

HERITAGE CIRCLE
(Elizabeth and John Denning)
Burghope Manor, Winsley
Nr Bradford-on-Avon, Wiltshire
022 122 3557
A consortium of country-house owners which promotes marketing schemes.

GUILD OF MASTER CRAFTSMEN
170 High Street
Lewes, Sussex BN7 1YE
07916 77374/5
Useful for NPs searching for craftsmen to do jobs ranging from touching up a lead statue to roof tiling.

COMMISSION FOR HISTORIC BUILDINGS AND ANCIENT MONUMENTS
(Formerly Historic Buildings Council)
25 Savile Row, London W1X 2BT
01 734 6010 Ext 684
This Department of the Environment agency gives grants to cover structural repairs and restoration of buildings of 'outstanding historic or architectural interest'. By structural they mean repairs (not improvements) to the roof, stonework, dry rot, etc. The owner is generally expected to put up at least fifty per cent himself and to open the house to the public for an agreed number of days or by appointment. These relatively rare grants are restricted to major capital repairs and are not available for running or maintenance.

NATIONAL HERITAGE MEMORIAL FUND
Church House
Great Smith Street, London SW1P 3BL
01 212 5414
Out of its substantial funds the body has been able to aid the preservation of (its own interpretation of) the national heritage. It gave £8 million towards Belton House (£4 million towards house, contents and land; £4 million to the National Trust as an endowment). It attempts to meet the price of important works of art so that they can be purchased by a British gallery, and not a foreign buyer. As it assists the entire spectrum of the 'national heritage', competition for its funds is high. An NP with an endangered species of bat nesting in his attic or with an important woodland on his acres probably has a better chance of being helped by this body than one with just a few crumbling Carolean walls. It will also give loans (sometimes interest-free) in extreme cases.

COUNTRYSIDE COMMISSION
John Dower House
Crescent Place
Cheltenham, Gloucestershire
0242 521381
Awards grants for tree-planting schemes. This is especially helpful now as many of the great house parks, including Capability Brown landscapes, were planted in the eighteenth century and the trees have run their natural course. Will also give grants to landowners who open their estates for nature trails and picnicking. Also gives towards capital expenditure on outdoor facilities such as loos and interpretation centres (NPspeak for information booths at houses open to the public).

LOCAL AUTHORITIES
Can give grants and loans on buildings, land and gardens they consider to be of historic interest. The extent and conditions of the grants are up to the discretion of the individual authorities. These special grants are subject to legislation separate from ordinary Local Authority Improvement Grants and are aimed as much towards aesthetic as practical improvements or repairs. However the chief priority of most local authorities is to maintain the town hall and other buildings they themselves own, so few NPs have succeeded in extracting money from them for their own crumbling domains.

SOTHEBY'S CONSERVATION COURSE
34/35 New Bond Street, London W1A 2AA
01 408 1100
A five-day course conducted each February for owners of fine and decorative art. Museum experts advise on conservation and restoration.

WYE COLLEGE
Ashford, Kent
0233 812401
NPs take their one-year gardens' management course here.

HERITAGE EDUCATION TRUST
St Mary's College
Strawberry Hill, Twickenham, Middlesex
01 892 0051
Helps owners to devise programmes for visiting schoolchildren which will enable them to understand the running of the estate. The purpose is to educate the current generation to appreciate country estates as part of the nation's heritage.

WORK

What's the use of money if you have to work for it?

■

Man and Superman GEORGE BERNARD SHAW

THE ARMY

The landless gentleman, i.e. the second or third son, joined the army if he didn't enter the church. The army was not as lucrative as serving God but there were notable exceptions, officers plundering the richer corners of the Empire. The self-made Lord Clive's share of the spoils of Plassey came to £234,000. In today's money that is £8 million.

Alas for the unenriched soldier, pillage is currently out of vogue. Looters now risk being shot by their own side as well as by the enemy. But there are compensations for today's NP warrior. In 1900 it was written that to serve as an officer in the Brigade of Guards or Household Cavalry one needed a minimum private income of £500 a year (today: £14,000) to subsidize the paltry pay. Otherwise it could be difficult keeping up with the Ponsonbys off the field of battle. As one impecunious officer wrote in his diary in 1890: 'It was not altogether agreeable to be seen drinking water at mess, while others were drinking champagne.' It is a measure of today's NPdom that only £2,000 a year is thought necessary as sufficient private means to subsidize mess bills in the smart regiments.

Officers get far better remunerated than they used to, though hardly enough to be 'comfortable'. Recently an officer who fainted in the parade ground was diagnosed by the regimental doctor as suffering from malnutrition. It transpired that he was having such trouble in paying the instalments on his Volvo, settling his wife's Harrods account and keeping up gentlemanly appearances, he was forgoing the luxury of food.

Many officers view their civilian counterparts with envy, reasoning that even if they make it to colonel, they will be clearing only £15,000 a year after tax. Consequently many NPs foolishly abandon the security of the regiment to 'conquer the City' or 'invigorate industry'. They soon discover, however, that there are sparse pickings in the 'Big Smoke' for those qualified only to kill. Regretting this manoeuvre into civvy street, the military NP grows to realize that the army at least maintains him in the marginal status of 'officer' and gives him licence to do what the British gentleman has always been best at – shooting and being shot at.

THE CHURCH

Since the Reformation, the younger sons of the landed aristocracy have traditionally been 'put into the church' to preach the word of God if they weren't put into the army to uphold the gospel of the state. Few objected to this particular vocation, for the church could provide as high a financial reward as a spiritual. Nor did the young clergyman have to wait until he was elevated from a bucolic parish to an affluent bishopric before he started to reap large dividends for shepherding his flock.

Alas, today's church holds neither the community status nor the temptations of Mammon to lure the NP into its fold. For many the purpose of the church – ministering to the troubled and needy – has been superseded by Freud and the Welfare State. The God Squad is perceived by a large body of opinion as being comforting upholders of ritual at best, and a fringe brigade of sanctified social workers at worst.

Furthermore, an unsanctified social worker probably has better pay. The clergy has had a greater drop in salary than any other profession in the country. The financial downturn of the Ministers of God started at the turn of the century. By 1943 the archbishop's income had fallen four-fifths to £84,000 in today's money. Bishops were down to £25,000 and vicars to a paltry £6,000.

Today after tax and national insurance deductions, most of the clergy earn less than a skilled labourer.

The church has already become a rare profession for upper- and upper-middle-class sons. One curate who attended theological college in the mid-seventies reports that only a hand-

1835

THE CLERGYMAN'S RANK & HIS SALARY

Vicar

One in ten received over £1,500 a year (today's money: over £34,000).

Bishop

£4,000 for some (today's money: £90,000 a year).

Archbishop of Canterbury

£19,122 not including his other incomes (today's money: £420,000).

In addition they all received residences in proportion to their celestial stations.

1984

THE CLERGYMAN'S RANK & HIS SALARY

Vicar

£6,450 gross (some get less). After tax: £4,500.

Bishop

£12,165 gross. After tax: £8,000.

Archbishop of Canterbury

£22,930 gross. After tax: £15,000.

ful of his fellow students were from public school. 'Even a generation ago it would have been at least fifty per cent,' he says.

It's not just the younger generation who've had a change of attitude. When one mother, ambitious for her brainy NP son, was informed by him, at the age of eighteen, that he'd been 'called by God' to the church, her shocked response to her husband was, 'Darling, where did we go wrong?'

TRADE: THE SHOCK OF THE NOUVEAU

In 1797 when a banker called Smith was made the first Lord Carrington, all the peers, except his sponsors, walked out of the House of Lords in protest against the ennoblement of a man in trade. Trade is an upper-class dirty word.

Historically the British aristocracy have deemed it noble to reap the bounty of one's land while doing nothing more than attending a few balls, gambling away some acres at whist or riding to the hounds. In the grand scheme of things other people were meant to indulge in the distasteful pursuit of money. In the British upper classes money always had to be sanitized by the passing of at least two generations before it became respectable.

No wonder that even in this century the sons and daughters of rich merchants have always done everything they could to distance themselves from Daddy's embarrassing activities. Sir John Ellerman, a German immigrant, made a fortune in Britain. At the height of his success he was worth £55 million (today's money: £880 million). When he died in 1937, did his son take over the family business? No. He became an academic, publishing learned works on the natural history of the rodent.

With such a deeply rooted tribal antipathy to the market-place, the upper-class English businessman is virtually a contradiction in terms. He is a half-caste: gentleman by birth, toiler by fate.

Oliver Wendell Holmes once said that a child's education should begin at least 100 years before he was born. If this is true, then NPs need wait until the next century before they will be properly prepared to take over industry. As it is, a salmon might just as well be expected to nest in trees as an NP happily assimilate into an office block. That is of course if the NP can get into one.

Even titled NPs now find their snob appeal which was once so marketable is fast diminishing. Ulster King of Arms John Brooke-Little says that before the Second World War, impoverished nobles could always find well-paid sinecures in the City as companies felt their status was enhanced by having a lord on their board. But according to the Institute of Directors this is no longer the case. A spokesman, Andrew Hutchins, says the marketability of titled non-executive directors started to go out in the sixties. 'Today firms want only titled directors with a sound commercial track record. The appointment of some obscure titled squire with no company experience in no way bolsters the confidence of the business community. Indeed, such a move is often counter-productive as those in the know will be less impressed than suspicious.

And all too often the firms that want to use an NP's title to enhance their company with a good name are the kind that end up tainting the NP with a bad one. A recent example is the sixth Earl Grey (the second was a British Prime Minister) who accepted a directorship of a chain of sex shops. No doubt the salary of £20,000 a year that came with the appointment was financially irresistible for the impecunious lord who lives on a boat. But the wages of sponsoring sin are heavy if you have a title. Before resigning he was pursued by the police and pilloried by the press. Though many will continue to associate the name Earl Grey with that upmarket brand of fragrant tea, those with a taste for scandal might long remember his lordship as THE PORNO PEER.

What are the other options, then, for penniless nobility? Despite what might be inferred from cynical newspaper columnists, no titled NP is going to replenish his depleted coffers attending the House of Lords. The daily attendance allowance is only £16 a day, which is to cover London travel and food expenses. On the submission of expenses, country-based peers can claim up to £24 extra for travel and overnight costs. As one NP said of her father, an unemployed baron who had lost his estate: 'He finds parliament more dignified than the dole, but says it doesn't pay as well.'

However, the sixth Earl of Munster's ascension to the peerage in 1975 was a financial godsend. The impecunious ex-army officer had never paid his National Insurance so he found he was not eligible for a pension. Friends had to carry the enfeebled Earl into the House of Lords every day until his death at the age of eighty-four because it was his only source of income.

So the NP, titled or not, must work to live comfortably. Historically an impoverished upper-class young man who didn't marry a supportive heiress might have governed a stretch of the Empire, commanded a regiment or ruled a bishopric. Not only were such appointments relatively easy to come by for the well-connected but they could also be financially rewarding. Not so today. The Empire no longer exists to govern, the army is difficult to enter and like the church its greatest rewards will hardly maintain the NP in a state of fraying gentility, let alone propel him into riches. But what other profession today does? Few that NPs know of. As they survey the job market, NPs count themselves lucky if they earn enough to keep a modest flat, never mind maintain a stately home.

Unfortunately for the NP the worst-paid professions are those he finds the most agreeable – the wine trade, publishing and the auction houses. 'We pay appallingly,' admits Nick Bonham of Bonhams Auctioneers. 'Even after ten years, few but the best get much more than £10,000 annual salary.' London residential estate agents don't pay their employees well either. John D. Wood paid an Oxford graduate £3,000 when he started off and by the third year his annual salary had risen by a mere £500. NPs have come to realize that prestigious and agreeable jobs are at a premium. And the premium they pay to have those jobs is a ludicrously low salary. In the labour market the NP knows he is little more than cheap commercial cannon fodder. One thirty-year-old aristocrat who is reduced to being a lodger in a remote London borough, works for Chestertons. 'By the end of the year I'll be lucky to clear £9,000,' he says. 'OK, I get paid more than a lot of people in this country, but unlike them, half of what I earn has to go towards buying and maintaining the smart clothes necessary for the company image. If for one week I wasn't up to sartorial scratch, I could well lose my job.'

Nor are plutocratic contacts a secure means of a young NP getting well remunerated. When Jocelyn Hambro asked his friend Roddy Dewe to employ his godson in his PR firm and Dewe consented, Hambro declared: 'Just pay him agricultural wages, Roddy.'

Yes, of course the NP can succeed and make money in a profession like merchant banking or insurance – if he's bright – but he no longer enjoys the historical privileges once accorded to the upper bracket. He is on the same competitive footing as the grammar-school or comprehensive graduate with the same qualifications. Indeed, the lofty pedestal of his background can be an actual disadvantage as young NPs know full well. Employers now look out for good degrees and hard application; they are indifferent to pedigrees and a smart education.

The Honourable Angus Ogilvy who works in the City. More honour in cutting down trees?
PHOTO: NORMAN PARKINSON/CAMERA PRESS

THE GENTLEMANLY CODE

The NP is a gentleman first, a businessman second. In commerce this is problematic. As a gentleman it was ingrained into him not to steal. But to expand a business means stealing someone else's market: bad form for a gentleman.

'Don't go into the City,' the 12th Earl of Airlie told his son Angus Ogilvy , 'it's full of crooks.' He advised him instead to follow a gentleman's course and become a forester on the family estate. No dishonour in cutting down trees.

Because he lives by the gentlemanly code, the NP assumes that others are living by it too. No more than a handshake should firm up a deal, he believes. Thus he is continually being ripped-off. Being a gentleman also means paying your due to the Inland Revenue and ignoring such tax dodges as offshore companies, which he disdains. They smack of a lack of patriotism. The gentleman definitely wants to make profits, but he shudders at being a profiteer.

LOSING GRACEFULLY

A familiar mistake of the NP is to make an unconscious equation between the rules of play and the rules of business.

The NP was brought up on civilized warfare – cricket, football and rugger – where not only were you penalized when you played dirty, you were even shunned by your own team. Better always to lose with grace than win without.

In business the NP soon discovers this rule does not apply. It's not how you play the game, it is whether you succeed. Negotiating deals, the NP finds, is not unlike playing tennis against John McEnroe. The NP soon comes to the cynical conclusion that few really care if you lie, cheat or steal in business. All that matters is you don't get caught.

Robin Birley, the stepson of Sir James Goldsmith, runs a fast-food business in London's West End. He thinks that even now a lot of the upper classes retain values incompatible with the realities of the modern world. 'When boys leave public school, many have a belief that it's all right to be a loser, so long as you act honourably and be seen to be one of the boys. But today people end up despising elegant failures – the sort who runs a wine business for social reasons and lets the enterprise collapse through inefficiency. That sort of thing must come to an end.'

CONDITIONING

However deep his desire to replenish the family coffers, there reside within the NP insidious commercial antibodies, spawned subconsciously from an archaic aversion to begriming his patrician hands with the open pursuit of money. At home the NP child

observed his role model: Father.

As far as little Hamish could see, Father never did much work besides mildly reprimanding the borough council for erecting pylons over his potato fields, penning indignant letters to the *Daily Telegraph* and questioning his estate manager about cases of fluke in his neighbour's cowherd. Little Hamish was not like other children who used to see their daddy leave the house by eight in the morning and return from the office at seven in the evening.

At school he was also sheltered from the imminent reality of commerce. As he romped over the green playing fields, he never suspected his time might be better spent perusing the pink pages of the *FT*. And though a master might have waxed eloquent on the monetarist theory of Friedman, the basic rules of trade was a subject deemed unfit for young Hamish's noble mind.

David Wainwright, who runs a thriving jewellery business believes the conditioning processes at public school (he left in 1974) are pernicious when it comes to trade. 'There was

a residual snobbery about commerce at my school, Wellington. So none of us knew how much trade affected everything around us. No one made us aware that there were countless people making money – sometimes losing it – over every material object around us, like the paper we were writing on and the pens we wrote with. Personally I think this lack of understanding and conditioned disdain for trade can be a costly disadvantage in later life for those who either become involved in commerce or who have to handle money. And who of us these days does not?'

Julian Tomkins, whose father was the British ambassador in Paris, owns a small business in London that makes sorbet. He shares many of David Wainwright's sentiments: 'I was brought up to believe there is something very nasty about money. To this day I hate haggling over price. When I come face to face with someone who doesn't share this aversion, I feel at a tremendous disadvantage because I am far more likely to concede in negotiation than fight for every last penny like a good businessman should.'

Sorbet manufacturer: Julian Tomkins, son of a British ambassador. *PHOTO: TRACY CHAMOUN*

OFFICE POLITICS

The NP might more safely manoeuvre through a minefield than successfully negotiate the pitfalls of office politics. In order to get on, he might well condescend to take an egalitarian line with his less socially rarified colleagues but all too often finds his overtures are met with indifference, sometimes hostility.

The Queen's English might be an asset on the parade ground but the NP finds it can be a liability when attempting to ingratiate himself with fellow executives from Crouch End and Romford.

It is true that some sectors of the marketplace *are* more sympathetic to the NP, like merchant banking, accountancy, property and insurance; yet others like the manufacturing and technology industries are often hostile to those from upper-class backgrounds. Nick Pickering of Rochester Recruitment, an executive employment agency, says a man who sounds and appears working-class is easier to place than an upper-class man with the same qualifications. 'The working-class and the lower-middle-class type is perceived to be more greedy and ambitious – altogether a better company person. The manner of the upper-class person works completely against him. Whether it is true or not, he is often thought to be arrogant, uncommitted and blasé. For him to survive and get on, it is important that he plays down any unconscious mannerisms and attitudes of his class.' (see 'Accent')

Pickering says it is best for the upper-class man to have his own money to invest because then he will be entering business at a high level where he will be above reproach (by definition this precludes all NPs). 'If the upper-class person has to work his way up like everyone else he will find in all probability his pathway to the top impeded by jealous colleagues on the lower and middle rungs. In tight working environments a lot of those with upper-class demeanours are singled out as butts and scapegoats.'

THE CURSE OF INSUFFICIENT INHERITANCE

It's an ironic twist of the NP's fate that a small inheritance can often make him poorer than no inheritance at all. A steady trickle of sovereigns from the family trust shields him from the indignity of *having* to work for his living. A job is an optional extra for these NPs, not a financial necessity. When they get given a desk in the City and they're jostled about by the heaving throng on the tube into Mansion House, they are assailed by such mutinous self-doubts as:

☞ *Why do I spend my day fighting futile office politics?*
☞ *Why am I wasting my youth in some soulless concrete tower block?*
☞ *How much longer can I endure the suburban prattle of my colleagues?*
☞ *Why do I suck up to bosses I loathe and despise?*

Failing to quell this subversive train of thought, the NP is often tempted to forgo the irksome routine of a nine-to-five altogether. But more usually he compromises, settling instead for some 'gentlemanly occupation', i.e. he becomes a wine merchant, publisher or antiques 'expert'. Though they reap small salaries and negligible prospects for advancement, NPs concur that at least such work is 'civilized'. But the financially bereft NP feels his only chance of making good is sticking to his City apprenticeship. This NP will stoically suffer any humiliation in order to advance his career. But in the end it's worth it. He is the allegorical tortoise who wins the race against the NP hare with an inheritance.

By his mid-thirties, Reginald Slowstart is a company director on a substantial salary, living in Chelsea. However, Milo Port-Dregs, who's existing off his wine merchant's salary and the dying dribble of his trust, is still living in Balham 'to afford to send little Torquil to Winchester'. Too late he discovers that his small inheritance was a cushion to lean against, not a bed in which to recline.

ENTREPRENEURS

Even the name is foreign. Yet the allure to NPs is obvious. It implies making a vast sum of money while doing very little to achieve it. After all, his ancestors just lived off the fat of the land.

NPs are not above greed. They are constantly on the lookout for a nice easy way to recoup their former stations. Yet they usually lack the inscrutable drive and cunning of their social inferiors who breed successful entrepreneurs like rabbits.

He suffers from one of two drawbacks. Either he is too eager and leaps blindly into an enterprise, losing his entire investment, or he is far too cautious. The cautious NP's attitude towards affiliating himself with a business is based on a similar criterion to that of associating with a person. He expects a proven track record of one and an irrefutable pedigree in the other. By the time he gets up the nerve to take the commercial plunge, either his rivals have established an unbudgeable foothold or the market is fully glutted. He fails to understand the basic rule of entrepreneurship: a successful entrepreneur must seize the opportunity *before* everyone else, not *after*.

There is a common illusion that members of the upper classes can enter and survive in any field of business. In fact, NPs themselves have from time to time foolishly believed this myth. The Duke of Devonshire's cousin, Ned Cavendish, hatched what should have been a sound business scheme. At the time of the Thames dock redevelopment in the seventies, he found a way of acquiring cheap scrap metal and transporting it by barge at negligible cost. For a month he did exceedingly well . . . until he came up against the Cockney river mafia: 'First they removed my full barge and replaced it with an empty one,' he says. 'As if that wasn't enough, they then warned me I'd be found floating in the river. They figured, "Here's a guy walking around with a plum in his mouth . . . let's take him on." The river also works on backhanders which I didn't understand.'

He realizes now that the way to have dealt with the situation would have been to hire some thugs to offer him protection and to facilitate pay-offs. But this would have gone against the grain. 'It doesn't come naturally to me to fiddle,' he explains. His river enterprise quickly folded. He now runs a business with more gentlemanly competitors – Bella Figura, a china ship in the Fulham Road.

INVERSE JOBBERY

Rather than face the aggravation of bolshy work colleagues, the undignified scrabble up the corporate ladder and the tedious routine of a solid career, many younger NPs have forsaken respectability and security and are poaching the domain of the traditional working class. They have become tradesmen, grocers, labourers, restorers, decorators, butchers, bakers and, if there was a demand for it, some no doubt would be candlestick makers.

Reaping the rewards of an expensive education: two ex-public schoolboys at work. *PHOTO: JODY BOULTING*

But this is not so much a desertion of background for NPs – it is more a return. Restoring antiques, wholesaling grouse and landscaping gardens is far closer to the NP's cultural identity than shuffling paper, flogging policies or calculating yields as a corporate hack. Anyway, these buccaneering NPs reason, downmarket jobs can be a lot more fun than being a drone in an office. Nor, does the NP rightly think, there will be much trouble or expense advertising – he just hands out his cards along with other NPs at drinks parties. Of course there will be a few psychological adjustments to make. When Mark Rudd decided to become a butcher, he fainted when he visited his first abattoir.

The only drawbacks for NPs who work in traditional downmarket jobs is the hostility they often encounter from the indigenous working classes. Decorators and labourers who enter builders' merchants with 'a plum in their marf are greeted with either derision or a simmering enmity. Most NPs on these occasions go the way of the Earl of Dumfries (part-time labourer) and speak a hybrid Cockney. When Julian Tomkins went to Covent Garden market to buy fruit for his sorbet enterprise, he found the peaches cost him ten times more than they should have done: 'They were obviously thinking that I was a toffee-nosed git who doesn't know what he's talking about, and I would pay anything they asked.' Tomkins's remedy is to employ a fruit agent. 'He's slightly more expensive but at least we're not getting ripped off,' he says.

Some NPs, however, candidly admit they choose a downmarket means of living because they feel they are not bright enough to succeed in a traditional career. One NP of fifty-one runs a newsagent's in Chelsea. The grandson of a highly decorated general, he says he wished he had 'done something proper' like being a lawyer or accountant, 'but I really don't think I am clever enough' he says. This NP, who requested anonymity, says his happiest days were in Africa where he was employed as an insurance rep. 'But now there is no Empire for people like me. Before the war I would have been sent out to run a tea plantation. Instead I run a newsagent's. I am just one of Britain's many displaced colonials.

'These days in Britain it's just not enough to do the right thing. To survive and prosper and keep a gentlemanly standard of living, you've got to have a brilliant brain,' he adds.

The newsagent says four of his customers were at Wellington with him. 'I haven't said anything to them and they obviously don't remember me as they haven't said anything either, or perhaps they do remember but they are too embarrassed. For thirteen years since I became a newsagent, I haven't seen any of my friends. I am so ashamed about how low I have descended, I have become a recluse.'

But with the conspicuous invasion of downmarket jobs by the upper and upper middle classes, many NPs now think virtually any occupation is acceptable so long as it's legal. Lord Simon Conyngham is the manager of an upmarket grocery in Belgravia called Mostly Smoked. 'Yes, I suppose I could go into the City,' he says 'but the money is not any better and I don't think I would enjoy it. Do I feel any shame? No, none at all. Today, there's no stigma attached to this sort of job.'

ADVANTAGES

TASTE NPs can spot a market that is invisible to most others: the *up*market. Their working-class predecessors were not always able to tune into what their upper-class customers wanted. As members of the upper class themselves, NP jobbers are uniquely qualified to cater to their social equals' tastes. NPs know what it's like to be on the receiving end of a silver tray of canapes, and because of this they understand that the presentation is just as important as the product.

'My background subjected me to a form of existence that was extremely pleasurable . . . and one where style counted for a great deal. Most of the catering in this country has been institutional. I want to pamper the rich,' says La Maison des Sorbets proprietor Julian Tomkins, great grandson of the Earl of Dudley.

Party Planner Lady Elizabeth Anson, who was raised at Shugborough, a stately home, has also brought to her clients the aesthetic sense indigenous to her kind. 'When I work in stately homes, I have a feeling about how they were lived in and how they *should* be lived in. The party should go on as if it was a hundred years ago,' she says.

FINANCING Some lucky NPs are able to wangle a couple of thousand pounds through family connections for start-up costs. Alternatively they can use the last dying splutter of the family trust to launch them in their new career. Julian Tomkins used his cache to pay the top patisserie in Paris to teach him the secrets of making good sorbet.

PUBLICITY NPs invariably get free publicity because of the newsworthiness of someone in their position getting his hands dirty. 'What's a nice peer like you doing in a place like this?' is the line the press takes with them. Lady Elizabeth Anson had to overcome her upper-class aversion to journalists. Once she began granting them interviews, her party business boomed. 'I've never had to spend more than £50 on advertising,' she says after two successful decades in business.

Articles on Julian Tomkins's sorbet factory have appeared frequently in the press. 'All the gratuitous PR is less because of the business than because of who I am,' he says.

NPs have a vast built-in market of family and friends. For Julian Tomkins, being well connected has not hurt business. Once he'd set up the sorbet machines on his Battersea premises the next move he made was to pick up the phone and give word of his new enterprise. 'Within three weeks the phone didn't stop,' he says. 'A lot of the business I've got has evolved purely from the fact that I knew a lot of people beforehand. People call up and say, "I know your parents. Will you do me a sorbet?" '

ENDORSEMENT

To endorse or not to endorse – that is the recurring NP question. As the NP surveys his decaying assets, is it any wonder he finds himself grappling with the dilemma of whether or not to lend his family name to a commercial product? The idea may be distasteful to him, yet where his grandfather would have been in a position to order mercantile scalliwags to the back door in no uncertain terms, the NP is reduced to seeking them out. Because so many NPs are coming out of the commercial closet, endorsing products has actually become an acceptable thing to do. But NPs are selective about what sort of products they would endorse. Pretty dresses would be on, but frilly underwear would not. The perverse law which governs these matters has it that the more risqué or disagreeable the product, the more money it stands to make the NP.

■

THE EARL OF NORMANTON has worked as a male model for rainwear manufacturer, Burberry and has allowed the EARL OF LICHFIELD to use his ancestral seat as a backdrop for photographing a nudie calendar.

■

LADY ELIZABETH ANSON has allowed her name to be associated with a line of glasses, linens and chocolates. 'I must believe in the product,' she insists.

■

THE EARL OF LICHFIELD uses the cachet of his name and position by emblazoning his initials on the inside of a line of American menswear to satisfy the label-hungry populace.

■

MARK PHILLIPS has had his riding sponsored by British Leyland. He opened his house to the public in order to promote Croft's Original Sherry.

■

PHOTO: DAFYDD JONES

PHOTO: JIM BENNETT/ALPHA

The Earl of Lichfield and Mark Phillips: not exactly *in* trade – but glad to endorse it.

LADIES' WORK

For NP Woman, a job is unavoidable, yet a career is distinctly unladylike. She thinks of her job as merely temporary whether or not that is the case. It is a vehicle which takes her from home and school to marriage and children. Her job may be boring, low-paid and unrewarding, yet because she never sees it as permanent, it never bothers her much. Any moment, Lord Right, lance firmly in hand, might bear down upon her and sweep her on to his white charger. Never mind that he is poorer than a church mouse and that she will have to remain working to keep the family in Stilton.

Because a job is temporary (or so she thinks) NP girl precludes any chances of earning the big money that could rescue her from being an NP for life. It is the rare upper-class woman who considers a serious career in finance, for instance. 'I know of only two upper-class professional women here in the City,' says Rosie Gibson, a Eurobond specialist at Samuel Montagu. 'Otherwise all the women come from middle- and lower-middle-class backgrounds.'

Miss Gibson thinks part of the reason must be upper-class chauvinism. 'I once had an Old Etonian boyfriend who took me to his parents' house in the country. My position as a merchant banker threw his parents and everyone else I met there that weekend. I think that having a woman in the room who could talk about blue-chip stocks upset their prescribed laws of social role-playing. I was made to feel a freak. With that sort of tribal attitude, it is no wonder few upper-class women go in for proper careers.'

Some NP women would disagree. They do have proper careers, they maintain – social careers. The NP girl's 'working' day begins at six o'clock in the evening, when everyone else's is ending. Other people wind down as the weekend approaches; the NP girl gears herself up. A job for young NP women is simply a means of bankrolling the serious business of gossipy parties and amusing weekends. So not for her the grimy portals of the Square Mile. Why clutter her mind with tin futures when tonight's dinner party looms so near? Why stay after business hours to discuss an important company deal? Work should never interfere with *real* life. Not for these aristocratic girls who toil as temps to pay for the evening taxis and weekend train fares the anticipation of a new challenge every day at the office. Work is just a drudge. 'I loathe going to a job every day,' gripes Fiona Irwin, the stepsister of an earl: 'I wasn't born to work.'

But eventually the unlikelihood of a royal prince or plutocratic peer whisking her away from the distasteful nine-to-five toil dawns on NP woman. Work is going to be a persistent blemish on her noble life. So NP woman has three courses of action:

— She takes up a serious career (rare)
— She doggedly continues down the same unexceptional path (common)

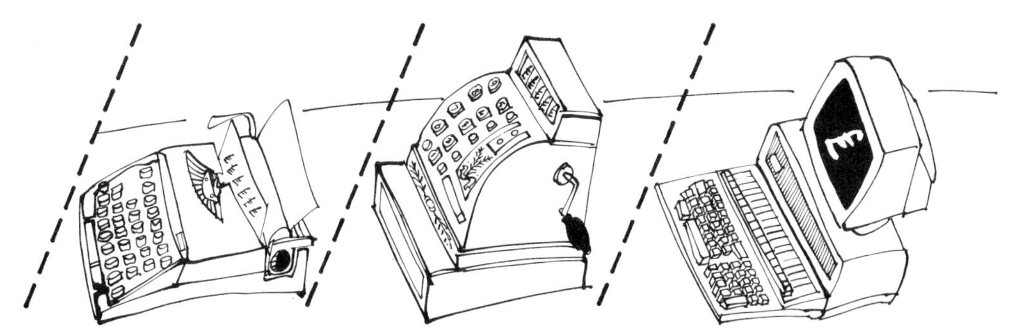

— She takes the radical step of starting up her own enterprise (less and less rare)

NP woman might not be financially sophisticated, but she is quite undaunted by the strains and perils of beginning a business. She squares up to its hurdles with the same plucky determination with which she braved those fences in the days of her childhood gymkhanas. Knightsbridge, Kensington and Chelsea seethe with NP women running small concerns. A social revolution is under way with upper-class women (like some of their men) invading the province of trade as restorers, caterers, grocers, dressmakers and decorators.

But though this is highly admirable (and the NP woman undoubtedly has more fun stippling walls than working as an anonymous minnow in a typing pool) it does little to redress her financial state. The NP woman, even more than the NP man, retains an instinctive aversion to money-grubbing.

One of the most successful NP women in trade is the already mentioned cousin to the Queen, Lady Elizabeth Anson, who runs the prestigious firm, Party Planners. 'I've never made much money,' she says wistfully. 'I'm a businesswoman as far as creativity and organization go, but the money side is the side I hate most. I would probably be ten times richer if I charged for things like overtime. But, as it is, I don't. Even my clients say I should charge more.'

As a lot of the business is conducted with her own kind, the NP woman is even more keen not to appear avaricious. She'll gladly soil her hands with peat moss or salmon mousse, but not pound notes. It's just 'not on' to be openly desirous of lucre. Mary Goodman, the wife of Tory MP Edward Leigh and great-granddaughter of Lady Ottoline Morrel, charges only £85 above the cost of material to make a ballgown to order. 'I would far rather charge under than over the commercial rate,' she says.

One of the problems facing NP girls is that as soon as they enter a trade they make it fashionable . . . and other NPs follow. Somebody at a London drinks party need only say he wants his walls dragged and a bevy of NP girls drape themselves around him trying to underbid each other. But the real casualties are not only fellow NPs, but all their other business rivals. One man in textiles commented that upper-class girls charge so little for silk screening and stencilling cushions, curtains and the like that established textile designers are either having to bring down their prices or look for a new career.

Yet NP girl announces what she does for a living with such supreme self-possession that few would suspect she is doing other than dabbling at a favourite hobby. If she declared she was a sewage operator no one would doubt the stateliness of the occupation. It's not that she's trying to make a grand impression. That's just how she sees herself.

GOOD WORKS

The traditional lady of the manor has for so long ministered to the needs of the community from within her cloistered portals that on becoming nouveau pauvre she often forgoes a well-paid job to continue striving for families which she imagines are less fortunate than her own. Often NP woman is not qualified to do anything *but* organize charities. And though her house may be in disrepair and outstanding bills long unpaid, the NP woman who goes out looking for a lucrative job often returns having either volunteered her services free to the local charity bazaar, or having landed a job in social welfare that hardly pays for the running of her rusting Volvo. One NP woman left a successful career as a designer to devote herself full-time to social work. 'I am unable to go after money *per se*,' she says. 'I would never be satisfied with my life if I pursued a selfish career.' NP woman always prides herself on transcending the insignificant details of her own life. Her situation has got bad, but hasn't Britain's got worse? she'll tell herself as she plays out her Lady Bountiful self-image typing and filing for organizations like Oxfam, Blackfriars Settlement, Citizens' Advice Bureau, WRVS and Age Concern.

Some of the Things an NP Girl Says She Does for a Living:

'I'm an interior decorator'
i.e. she wields a paintbrush
'I design ballgowns'
i.e. she's a seamstress
'I work at Belville Sassoon's'
i.e. she's a shop girl
'I do directors' lunches'
i.e. she's a skivvy
'I'm the chairman's PA'
i.e. she's a typist
'I manage a gallery'
i.e. she hangs pictures

Landscape gardener and dental hygienist: Lord and Lady Kenilworth. *PHOTO: DAFYDD JONES*

The Unusual Range of Work Undertaken By Today's Aristocracy

THE NOB	THE JOB
The Honourable Diana Maxwell	Playboy Bunny
Lord Fermoy	Bookbinder
Countess of Mar	British Telecom saleswoman
Lord and Lady Macdonald	Hebrides hoteliers
The Honourable Tony Monson	Pirate radio disc-jockey
Marquess of Queensbury	Potter
Lord Teviot	Bus conductor
Lady Kenilworth	Dental hygienist
The Honourable Patrick Sinclair	Bus driver
Lord Loughborough	Policeman
Earl Nelson	Policeman
Lord Strathnaver	Policeman
Lord Kingsale	Silage-pit builder
Nevinson de Courcy (Kingsale's heir)	Municipal drains inspector
Marquess of Kildare	Landscape gardener
Lord Kenilworth	Landscape gardener
Lord Simon Conyngham	Delicatessen assistant
Viscount Boyle	Waiter
Lord Blackford	Waiter
Lady Kathleen Pelham-Clinton-Hope	Hong Kong night-club waitress
Earl Grey	Sex-shop chain director
Lord Colwyn	Dentist
Viscount Southwell	Travel agent
Earl of Dumfries	Labourer
Marquess of Tweedale	Labourer
Viscount Molesworth	Clerical worker
Lady Megan Edgecumbe	Plymouth council gardener
Earl of Ypres	Hall porter
Lord Northesk	Isle of Man jewelsmith
Baroness Sharples	Pub landlady
Earl of Breadalbane	Pub piper
Count Zygmunt Zamoyski	Refuse-collector

LIFESTYLE

POOR OR LESS

The NP is bred to appreciate the best things in life, yet not have a nervous breakdown if he can't afford them. As long as he can live his life with what he considers to be the basic necessities, he is content. Why drive a Rolls-Royce when a Peugeot Estate has more room for dogs and is a tenth of the price? Why spend £60 switching on the castle's central heating when a two-hour walk will warm him up for free?

If today's upper classes spot an opportunity to save money, even at the expense of bodily comfort, they will seize it. Celebrated show-jumping baronet Sir Harry Llewelyn knocked out all the baths in his Welsh mansion and installed ones half the size. Why? To save on hot water.

Nor do the upper classes disdain the welfare state. Doctor Rossdale, a physician with a private practice in the London borough of Kensington says his list of patients read like Debrett's when he started over twenty years ago. Most of them, he says, have now forsaken him for the National Health. Today, Americans and corporate executives compose the bulk of his patients.

Financially, NPs have an advantage over other classes because they feel no insecure compulsion to acquire modern symbols of material status. That is because the only status they are prepared to acknowledge is social and that, they feel, they have in abundance. A Wandsworth bus conductor might feel he is bettering himself buying the latest video and hi-fi. Not so his next-door neighbour, Sir Roland Rightoff. Sir Roland will settle for a gramophone and black and white television and furthermore he will boast of acquiring them at a knock-down price at the sales. This sort of saving can mean Sir Roland can, perhaps, afford to be a 'gun' on a small shooting syndicate in Hampshire, or, like so many NPs, he can invest surplus cash in an Education Trust for his children. Alternatively he might spend a windfall topping up his cellar with good claret, getting fitted for a Savile Row suit and replacing some frayed shirts in Jermyn Street. The essential style of the NP's life never changes; it either intensifies or slackens, depending on the current state of his bank account.

It can cost little to be an NP in a state of truncated gentility. We calculate the bottom line for capital set-up costs as £45,000. Thereafter the NP needs a minimum of £6,000 a year net to survive with a modicum of dignity (and many do not). For the NP who does not have £45,000 capital, he or she should add £120 on to their yearly income requirement for every £1,000 they lack. This is the twelve per cent interest that would have to be paid on a mortgage from a bank or building society: if the NP had only £25,000, he would need to make £8,400 net of tax a year; if the NP had absolutely nothing, he or she would need £11,400 net income.

CAPITAL SET-UP COSTS

A three-roomed maisonette in Parsons Green	£38,000
Furniture from Bonhams (Lots Road) and Habitat	£2,000
Linen, cutlery and crockery from Peter Jones	£1,500
Prints and a couple of oils from Christies, (South Kensington)	£1,000
Rugs, carpets, curtains and decoration	£2,200
One black and white television and cheap hi-fi	£250
Bicycle (from police auction of unclaimed stolen goods)	£50
TOTAL:	£45,000

YEARLY OUTGOINGS FOR THE NP

THE FLAT

Rates	£350
Electricity	£200
Gas (central heating and hot water)	£400
Telephone (make most personal calls from the office)	£250
Renovation, redecoration, upkeep	£100
Plumbing and electrical maintenance	£50
Household goods (loo paper etc. bought in bulk with friend's Cash and Carry card)	£350
TOTAL:	£1,700

HER EXPENSES

Hairdresser (she economizes by only getting it cut there)	£70
Shoes	£90
Make-up and scent	£85
One evening dress and designer outfit (from second-hand shop)	£140
One hat (from M & S)	£15
Spending money (presents for nephews and nieces)	£300
Basic clothes and accessories (opaque tights that don't ladder so fast)	£300
TOTAL:	£1,000

HIS EXPENSES

Country membership of a London club	£120
One suit (from Harrods sale)	£110
Shirts and ties (from M & S)	£90
Shoes and shoe repairs	£80
Haircuts	£30
Basic clothes	£200
Spending money (for the odd charity ball double ticket)	£370
TOTAL:	£1,000

COMMON EXPENSES

Fortnight's holiday in Scotland (cadging off friends)	£250
Laundry and dry-cleaning	£150
Train, tube and occasional taxis	£600
Newspapers, magazines, books and records	£200
Food	£800
Restaurants, wine bars and pubs	£900
Drink	£400
TOTAL:	£3,300

GRAND TOTAL FOR SINGLE NP OF EITHER SEX: £6,000

TRANSPORT

Gone are the days when ladies and gentlemen would parade down Rotten Row showing off the contours of their latest brougham or phaeton. Practicality and economy are the only requirements for today's upper classes. Aesthetically speaking, the scruffier the vehicle the better, which is fortunate for the NP as his spending power puts him right in the height of fashion.

The attitude of NPs to expensive cars and those who drive them is accurately encapsulated in one of their favourite jokes: Q. 'What's the difference between a hedgehog and a Porsche?' A. 'The hedgehog has its pricks on the outside.' Geddit?

NPs are even dismissive about Rolls-Royces: 'Even if I *could* afford a Rolls-Royce, I'd never buy one' they are often heard to say. They have even pegged the premier car 'Roller' as if to disparage the mechanics of the machine by inferring it's not much better than a marble. To justify their scorn, NPs exchange derisive stories about the rare instances of a recalcitrant Roller.

Most employed NPs don't have much choice in what car they drive. Their companies decide for them. This usually finds them victims of a Buy British policy which is upsetting for the NP as he thinks it smarter to drive a foreign VW Golf than his firm's Ford Fiesta. But even in town he feels it is all right to drive a naff motor so long as it faintly resembles an estate car – i.e. slightly splattered with mud (country lanes), animal hair all over

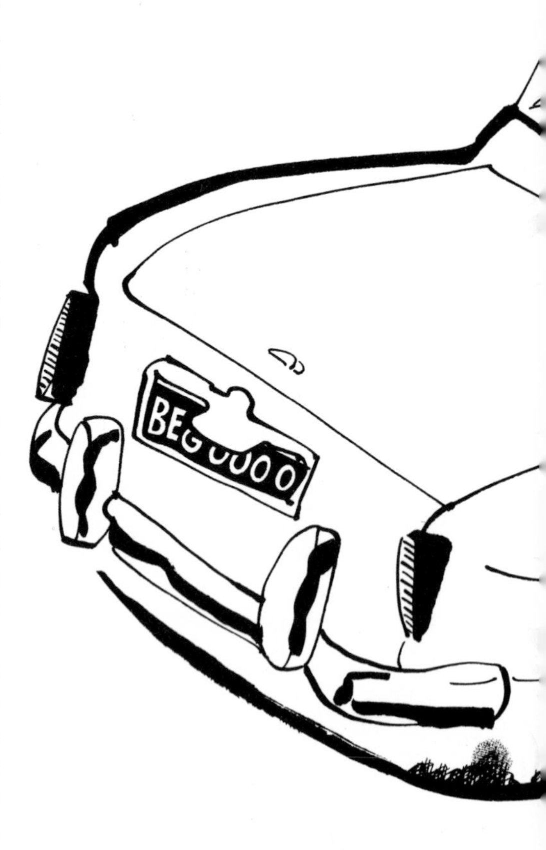

the back seat (panting gundogs), and an empty cartridge rolling on the floor (rough shooting at the weekend). To make it undeniably clear that he belongs to the upper bracket an NP might well have prominently displayed on his windscreen a Guards Polo Club sticker, or failing that, a point-to-point sticker.

Most NPs can't afford proper estate cars (at least, not new ones) so they usually buy a Mini Metro, VW Golf or Renault 5. 'They're good v for m' or 'so much easier to park' is the NP line. The more downmarket the car the better. NPs have been heard to say, 'It lowers the risk of kidnapping.'

Smart young London NPs have accorded their patronage on Motortune. One NP thinks them so chic he sports a Motortune sticker on his wheelchair. Another popular dealer (but small) is Simon Martyn in Queensgate Place Mews.

In town many NPs have given up cars altogether and some try to save money on the tube by riding bicycles to work 'purely to keep fit'. Female NPs rarely like to admit they are taking 'a slow red' (bus) for some appointment because they are too broke to afford 'a fast black' (taxi). Their oft-repeated rationale for travelling by this one mode of transport they can afford is that 'it's so nice to meet the general public' as if they're on some anthropological excursion. What they seem to forget is that as NPs, they, too, are now the general public.

THE NP AND HOLIDAYS

FOLLOWING THE DEBT SET

Travel is one of the last luxuries any NP will sacrifice. The lure of foreign lands is in the NP's bones and its perils make it all the more challenging. Didn't his great-great-grandfather get dysentery on The Grand Tour? Wasn't his great-aunt speared as she dug for fossils in the Congo?

Today's travel opportunities are fraught not so much with danger as annoying inconveniences. The Riviera and the Algarve are not only extortionately expensive but are teeming with his own country's lower orders reeking of Non-U items such as Worthington E and malt vinegar. Five-star hotels are merely stars in his eyes. But NPs have mastered the art of reciprocation. 'My place is yours, your place is mine' is the motto for those who still have a place. Cultivating friends with sumptuous villas or palaces abroad, the NP endlessly invites them to stay at his damp and draughty pile in the shires. As the unwary guests say their goodbyes, the NP host discreetly bids them sign his visitors' book. Then if a reciprocated invitation to the guest's Tuscan villa is not soon forthcoming, the miffed NP can phone him, bemoan the absence of his company, mention he'll be in Florence next week and wonder if he could drop by . . .

When he knows he will be staying in the sort of environment which his genes crave, he won't mind suffering the multitudes of camera-clad tourists on a charter flight or being stepped over by leather-thonged holidaymakers as he sleeps on the floor of the train.

When he is abroad the NP doesn't mind discomfort, indeed some NPs relish it. It introduces an atavistic spirit of adventure while at the same time making them feel they are 'travellers' rather than 'tourists'. 'Tourists' have connotations of cossetting and pre-organized packages, 'travellers' of being trail-blazing pioneers, which is more appropriate to the NP's noble temperament.

As a rule NPs prefer an eccentrically run family hotel to an air-conditioned Hilton. They'd drive twenty miles to a deserted cove rather than step out on to a congested beach next door. The company of an indigenous inhabitant they can't understand is preferable to a Manchester computer salesman they can. The NP abhors 'resorts'. The ones catering for his class he cannot afford and he didn't travel a thousand miles to spend a fortnight with his neighbourhood grocer at one that he can.

Tripoli, the capital of Libya, might not be everyone's idea of a fun holiday destination, but Richard Partridge, a gentleman farmer from Dorset, took his wife there on a ship due to be scrapped. Requiring a small crew to cook and assist as deck hands, a company hired the couple to travel on the ship's last voyage from Holland. Their duties were light and having travelled round France, Spain and into the Mediterranean, they were both given a substantial fee plus their air tickets back home. 'It was good to get away,' says Mrs Partridge. 'I had never seen the Mediterranean before and naturally it was delightful to have made a profit out of the whole adventure.'

MORE BOSH THAN POSH

In the old days when the upper classes travelled to India, the steward always arranged it that their cabin faced the morning sun. So – it is said – the deckhands coined a new name for these discriminating passengers – posh, the letters of which stood for 'Portside Out, Starboardside Home'. Recently a waggish NP described his new station as a traveller as 'bosh' – 'Bucketshop Out, Standby Home' he explained.

Today it seems even the royals are more bosh than posh. Not only do many of them not pay to travel first-class, they don't even pay the scheduled fare for economy. The new Thomas Cook for the royals is the poignantly named Empire Travel, a cut-price travel agency in Southall, Middlesex, which recently arranged flights for Viscount Linley and the Duke and Duchess of Kent to Nepal.

But unless they are very grand, few NPs can rely on receiving the same treatment as Viscount Linley, who at Heathrow Airport was ushered into the VIP lounge and then flown off in the luxurious Clipper Class section of the plane which normally costs £600 extra. 'The Tourist Class was overbooked,' claim Pan Am, who thus demonstrate the more traditional usage of the word 'bosh'.

NP HOLIDAY CHOICE

Where They Go

FRANCE
(but not Riviera)

ITALY
(perpetually collapsing lire very attractive)

IRELAND
(near a good salmon river)

SCOTLAND
(on a friend's moor)

CORNWALL
(in a rented farm house)

INDIA
(at a Maharajah's palace)

KENYA
(most NPs have had relations there and a lot still do)

TURKEY
(unspoilt and adventurous)

THAILAND
(if they can afford the cost of flight)

MOROCCO
(might even settle there if homosexual)

PORTUGAL
(but not the Algarve which is too expensive and very flash)

Where They'd Rather Not

ST TROPEZ
(unless in grand villa)

UNITED STATES OF AMERICA
(money is class there, so NPs fear they'd be despised)

GREECE
(very spoilt and vulgar now but might go on a yacht or if friends owned an island)

SCANDINAVIAN COUNTRIES
(Dull and booze very expensive)

GERMANY
(DM too strong)

USSR
(clan loyalty to the Romanoffs)

THE WEST INDIES
(the playground of the Nouveaux Riches)

COSTA DEL SOL
(playground of grocers)

ALCOHOL

It is the rare NP man who doesn't have a congenital fondness for alcohol. It is the balm to wash away his sorrows; it is the valium for his despair. Is it any wonder then that he occasionally overdoses on his ancestral medicine and gets incapably plastered? He never reprimands himself too harshly, though, rationalizing that he'd be something of a class traitor if every so often he didn't get as drunk as a Lord.

The NP drinker is inherently suspicious of the teetotaller, believing that he must either be Muslim, a member of Alcoholics or Narcotics Anonymous or in mid-cure of a venereal disease. He dismisses any argument that the person may not actually like alcohol as tripe, and refers in mocking tones to teetotallers as 'ginless wonders'.

But the NP finds it a sad fact that he can't afford the wines and spirits consumed so profusely by his forbears. He well remembers the story of the Duke of Wellington leaving his false teeth to soak in a glass of good port every night till morning and reflects that if the Iron Duke did the same with some of the rot-gut *his* palate was forced to endure, by dawn they would have disintegrated. Whereas his ancestors had ample opportunity to display taste in their choice of Chateau and grape, the NP feels the only use for his discriminating eye is to check the vodka label to make sure he is not being diddled on proof percentage.

Yet despite his diminished finances, the NP still retains some admirably discerning standards – even when scraping the bottom of the bin end.

CHAMPAGNE

Now that the nouveaux riches have put their stamp of approval on Dom Perignon, it is conspicuously out with the NP set – not that they could afford it anyway. 'I don't really like bubbly,' they'll claim, 'not good for the head, old boy!' This attitude, however, does not deter the NP from accepting so many glasses of the stuff from the proffered silver tray at weddings and official freebie functions. When the NP does dip into his pocket to purchase a case or two of fizz, he usually purchases Supermarket Sparkling Wine. Studiously concealing the label with a white cloth, he congratulates himself on serving bubbly that could just about be taken as a medium-priced champagne.

WINE

NPs have made the serving of plonk not only acceptable but in polite society *de rigueur*. 'Have a glass of plonk,' they'll suggest, stressing the last word in such a way that you fear you have been embarrassingly remiss in not ever having tasted this distinctive chateau called 'Plonk' before. Actually the word is probably mischosen. The standard NP dinner party offering is better than plonk – about 50p better.

On the whole NPs are not label-conscious, having traded in that ancient snobbery for a more economical reassessment of the item's intrinsic value. Chateau Yquem is perhaps the greatest of the sweet wines, but NPs now opt for Muscat de Beaumes de Venise at a third of the price. And as NPs tend to drink by grape or region rather than chateau, it would not be surprising to hear an NP say, 'This Hungarian wine far exceeds its closest French rival.' Cabernet Sauvignons and Spanish Riojas are particular favourites of NP cognoscenti. Indeed the NP will experiment with wines that have rarely been heard of in traditional dining rooms, let alone drunk: Chilean, Argentinian, Bulgarian and Australian have all now been served (though usually decanted first) to many unwitting wine snobs. The NP has even forgiven the Germans for the last two major wars because of their drinkable Rieslings.

But there are occasions when the NP decides a respected wine is called for. Conveniently he has an uncle with a vineyard in Tuscany, a brother-in-law called Rothschild, or an old school chum in the wine trade. But even at wholesale prices he has to save up by drinking supermarket cider for a month beforehand.

NPs occasionally dabble in wine kits 'just to experiment, old boy – wouldn't actually drink the stuff!' they'll lie. Usually it is just for home consumption, which is just as well, but there are times when the destitute NP is driven to desperate measures. When the credit cards have had to be returned and the local off-licence demands cash on the nail, NPs have been known to serve their decanted home brew, Maisonette Parsons Verhde. Actually NPs usually serve cheap red because it not only tastes better but, fortified with a liberal dose of cooking brandy, it's nearly palatable. 'I just love this peasant wine,' the NP has been heard to enthuse, 'it reminds us of our old place in Tuscany.' After the second glass, it is said, guests no longer trouble themselves over the nectar's unfathomable provenance, but they do wonder why they have such a throbbing hangover the following morning.

Among NPs it is perfectly acceptable to start pernicious rumours that are self-benefiting. One such rumour has launched a pervasive fad: NPs have pronounced that boxed wine is 'quite all right'. Some of this poisonous fluid has seeped into (horrors!) the drawing-rooms of the Old Wealth. Who knows to what depths NPs will drop next? News had it that recently in Fulham – prime NP stomping ground – the grander housewives were ordering Cotes de Tarn from their Unigate milkman!

When it comes to English wines, the NP along with the rest of the world laughs at the absurdity of imbibing his native elixir. The reality is that he would not object to drinking it if the prices were lowered in line with plonk from other countries.

WHISKY

NPs claim they 'don't care a sod' about the brand of whisky they drink. They rationalize cheap brands by protesting that 'no one can tell the difference, especially in London, where the water is so hard'. But the stigma that NPs risk by serving cheap whisky warrants their decanting it. Caddish NPs buy Sainsbury's own label whisky which they then pour into Famous Grouse bottles.

VODKA

Only supremely uneducated NPs buy anything other than their local off-licence's brand. NPs know that the vodka one buys in Britain is rarely made with potatoes, but with grain, making it nothing more than flavourless gin. 'The price reflects the advertising budget,' NPs are heard to quip smugly. NPs laughed derisively at an absurd advertising campaign in the upmarket glossies which displayed a family tree of misers who bought cheaper vodka than the preposterously priced brand label Smirnoff.

GIN

Unlike vodka, it is not acceptable yet to have a supermarket gin on one's drinks tray. A residual snobbery remains with gin so NPs uncharacteristically stick to the expensively branded Gordons and Beefeater.

CIDER

Tempted by the 89p price tab at Waitrose, the NP first buys cider 'just to braise the loin of pork, old boy!' If he is destitute the transition from Beaujolais to Bulmers is quick. Many dinner guests of NPs now grow increasingly perturbed as they find themselves contributing 'jolly good wine' to a meal where the host has seen fit to provide a couple of bottles of fermented apple juice.

BEER

NPs mostly drink beer in pubs in the country, where they can demonstrate the Common Touch by mixing with tramplike but usually richer yokels. The NP always orders the pungent local brew, despite its tasting as if a couple of rats had a hand in the fermentation. This gives him a feeling of belonging to the area, a poignant sentiment for the NP as the area once belonged to his grandfather.

At home the NP maintains these rustic pretensions by offering guests real ale like Ruddles. Occasionally, he'll thrust a glass of alarmingly smoky liquid at them and insist they give their opinion. Few give it honestly as what they have in their hand is the result of the NP's first experiment with a Boots DIY beer-making kit.

MIXERS

The NP no longer gets his tonic and soda from Scchhhh, you know who, but from a Heath Robinson contraption called Soda-stream. Powered by gas, this unlikely piece of modern technology saves the NP ten pounds a month. Alas, if only he could get the mixes right and remember to lug the empty gas cylinder back for a refill!

PUNCH

This is a good excuse for NPs to dispose of all that vile liqueur they were given for Christmas by their eccentric relations. As an after-thought they add generous rations of tea, cinammon sticks, orange juice and whatever else is mouldering in the pantry. An NP punch is an alcoholic last resort.

FOOD

Just because they are no longer rich doesn't mean NPs have forfeited the traditional fare of their ancestors: they just usually wolf lobster and truffles at someone else's expense. Should you be served salmon at an NP household, you can be sure that it was landed at their Uncle Rory's estate in Inverness, not the fish counter at Harrods. The same applies with pheasant and partridge. The NP's deep freeze is a treasure trove of game slaughtered by rural relations.

But the food-buying habits of the upper classes have perceptibly changed. W.E. Miller, a butcher's in Chelsea Manor Street, report that a lot of their posher clients now forgo expensive cuts of steak and buy instead Crown Roast and Fillet End. A nearby fishmonger says that where upper-class customers used to think nothing of buying dozens of oysters and pounds of smoked salmon, today, many of them come into his shop only to buy 'salmon bits'.

The only time most upper-class NPs eat caviar now is at thrashes hosted by the rich. Certainly the nouveaux pauvres never buy it. However they are not averse to spending 89p on a small jar of its ersatz equivalent, lumpfish roe. But NPs never try to con unwitting guests that it is Sevruga or Beluga. They either plaster it over cheese dips or sparsely distribute it in plates of consommé – a poor nob's gourmet dish called 'Parrot's Eye'.

NPs coming from the country invariably make an excursion to Fortnums or Harrods, if only to stock up on annual rations of Gentleman's Relish. But for those London-based NPs, Gervase and Drusilla Hardup, the corner shop is an adequate emporium. Here, they can chat good-naturedly with the proprietor, paternalistically nodding as he fulminates on local community problems. The anonymity imposed by supermarkets speaks too audibly of new-fangled mass production. At any rate, the absurdity of queueing up with the masses for the sole purpose of saving a mere 4p on a pound of tomatoes is too humiliating even for their reduced circumstances. The two notable exceptions to their disdain of supermarkets are Sainsbury's and Waitrose. Both cater for upmarket tastes at downmarket prices, stocking mandatory NP provisions like quails' eggs, breast of duck and fresh pasta. Drusilla finds Waitrose's line of pre-scraped and chopped fresh vegetables a special boon, enabling her to spend more time at closing-down sales.

Although London NPs profess to dislike 'rip-off' late-night supermarkets, they are often spotted there at eight in the evening, counting out their pennies for some overpriced plonk or taramasalata on their way to a dinner party in Pimlico.

EATING OUT

'I did have money once. But like a lot of young men from my background, I blew it on wining and dining. Wining and dining is an easy way to blow a lot of money quickly.'

LORD SIMON CONYNGHAM

Being content at home, most older NPs venture out to restaurants a mere once or so a month. Their close dinner-party circuit provides the necessary outlet for social intercourse. They never treat going out to a restaurant as if it's a big occasion. To celebrate a minor anniversary an NP couple might well go to Wheelers or Bill Bentley for two dozen oysters and a bottle of champagne. They weep no tears at not being able to afford the saucy foreign food of the Gavroche.

At the tail-end of an NP drinks party a host might suggest going out for a meal. Among these NPs is an unspoken understanding that the local cheapy ethnic (Italian, Chinese or Indian) will do. Impromptu Bacchic banquets are as remote from NPs as Ancient Greeks.

Younger NPs (especially singles in rented flats) often need to seek refuge from their dreary domiciles. Lothario bachelors who might be content to stay at home are under what they consider unfair social pressure to feed their dates on neutral territory, so they, too, go out to restaurants a lot. So debilitating is this to their pockets that many are forced to pay with accumulated luncheon vouchers. Thomas Tightwad winces when Melissa Moderate orders liver at £4 which he knows he could have cooked back at his flat for 40p. He takes girls to La Bersagliera in the King's Road (noisy but good cheap pasta) or Bistro Vino (palatable at palatable prices) or Tootsies (trendy hamburger joint).

However, when wanting to impress, he'll whisk his intended to Langans or Le Caprice

Delicatessen manager: Lord Simon Conyngham.
PHOTO: TRACY CHAMOUN

where he will order two starters or the main course only. Polite young ladies know the form well, and are compliantly abstemious.

Not having the same compulsion to keep up smart appearances, country-based NPs spend less when they eat out. Few, however, are prepared to be as enterprising as Lord Kingsale who dines regularly at his local Somerset hostelry in return for fixing and maintaining the pub's plumbing.

NON-NP RESTAURANTS NPs studiously avoid any restaurants whose names begin with 'Quality' (always denotes the opposite) and 'San' – where rich socialites mingle with their chroniclers. 'Chez' and 'Villa' imply a familiarity with the proprietor that NPs are unwilling to risk. They shun all steak houses, though they don't shun steak. One would never hear an NP announce: 'Let's go to Wimpy's or Burger King.' However, Big Macs appeal to his sense of the ridiculous and his wallet. He'd never frequent the Upper Crust, a Knightsbridge tourist-trap specializing in pies, not peers. He once made the mistake of going to Drone's where he lingered over a bowl of chili and delivered 'clever' asides about the assorted spivs, climbers and would-be starlets 'just in from LA'.

NP RESTAURANTS

Kettner's: NPs approve of its theatrical bordello interior

Comolario: Unpretentious food, ambience and prices

MacDonald's: The only hamburger chain acceptable to NP standards

Blue's Trattoria: Local spaghetti house for Fulhamites

Annabelle: Not to be mistaken for its near namesake (though it sometimes is by unwary NP girls) NP girls bring the wine; NP boys pay for corkage and meal

Pizza Express: NPs fulfil *noblesse oblige* by ordering the Venetian pizza (10p goes to the Venice in Peril Fund)

Le Caprice: NPs sit at the bar where lunch prices are cheaper

Tootsie's: One step up from MacDonald's

Polish Hearth Club: NPs admire the Polish NPs' dignity as well as the Slav cooking

Parsons: Spaghetti and hamburger parlour for NPs visiting the Fulham ABC cinema

La Bersagliera: Italian pasta parlour for younger NPs

Foxtrot Oscar: Trendy hamburger joint for young marrieds

Bistro Vino: A v. popular NP chain

King's Road Jam: NP patronage decreases as prices increase

L'Artiste Musclé: A Mayfair restaurant with a 'Left Bank' atmosphere (and prices)

Stock Pot: Heavily frequented by NPs during Harrods sale

Toad of Toad Hall Pooh Corner: Fun slumming south of the river

Asterix: Where NPs get pancaked on cheap Normandy cider

The Chelsea Kitchen: Probably the cheapest nosh in bun-throwing distance of Sloane Square

Khan's: Very trendy Indian restaurant in Westbourne Grove

The Picasso: The London NP's answer to the Deux Margots

Strikes: A hamburger chain that is a favourite with country NPs in London who want to give their children a 'treat' (quarter the price of Fortnum's)

Sea-Shell of Lisson Grove: Chic fish and chip shop. NPs bring their own wine as they don't charge corkage

The Red Stall on Chelsea Bridge: Broke NPs get hot-dogs and hamburgers here. Not exactly cordon bleu, but very good view

THE NP & HIS SOCIAL LIFE

'Yes, I find an advantage in being a Lord, even a poor one. If I am sitting at a dinner party and I fart very loudly, everyone thinks it eccentric and a bit amusing. If anyone else did the same, they'd say it was gross and vulgar.'

▪

LORD KINGSALE,
Premier Baron of Ireland

NPs' mantelpieces are perennially adorned with ticked invitations aligned with architectural precision. Yet few of these 'stiffies' (upper-class argot for invitations) are to the grander balls and more opulent dinner parties. His inability to reciprocate means for most NPs a cruel exclusion from the lavish social circuit of Britain's ancien riche.

But many PR men, businessmen and foreign ambassadors believe NPs add aristocratic distinction to gatherings and bombard them with entreaties to attend wine tastings, gallery openings, first nights and embassy cocktail parties. Yet NPs invariably respond with offence at the suggestion that they build their lives around free events. Indeed, they claim they are highly selective about whom they will honour with their exalted presence. 'I'm not one who will go anywhere for a free drink or meal like some royals I know,' fumed one NP. Yet without freebies most NPs know they would be condemned to a homebound exile.

WINE TASTINGS

The most eagerly awaited NP freebie is the wine tasting. At these gatherings, the NP can be witnessed wending his way round the various vintages with an authoritative air making voluminous notes on the merits of labels he could never afford and shamelessly disregarding the spittoons placed strategically to keep the serious connoisseur's palate clear.

This exercise helps to create the illusion that some day, if ever the wines were up to his inestimable standards, he might deign to honour the proprietor with a purchase. Rare NPs do occasionally buy the odd case to insure keeping on the invitation list. In the long run, they reason, they get more than they ever have to pay for.

EMBASSY PARTIES

With their old-world protocol and lavish spreads, most embassy parties provide the right sort of nostalgic ambience for NPs. Arriving at these colossal edifices that were once the private residences of his ilk, the NP feels that he has come home. For an evening the NP can roam the corridors and reception rooms, sentimentally recalling the far-off time when his own kind reigned supreme in such a house and not some distasteful government representative.

In return for this masochistic glimpse of the past the NP gratefully provides his distinguished hosts with gossip, lifted from Messrs Hickey or Dempster, erudite political analysis, gleaned from the *Spectator* (or the *Economist*) and epigrams from a Penguin anthology.

FIRST NIGHTS

NPs never get invited directly to the first night of a play or film. Rather they are brought along as social ballast by showbiz patrons. At the party afterwards NPs are liable to offend the cast unwittingly by neglecting to pour lavish praise on the production no matter how impressive it was. Gushing flattery simply runs contrary to the NP's understated nature.

GALLERY OPENINGS

NPs defensively claim that they would never attend a gallery opening merely for the free plonk. They would, they insist, accept only an invitation to a Belgravia or St James's opening. At the gallery the NP seldom actually looks at the pictures – save, perhaps, throwing one or two supercilious glances – he is too busy criticizing the inferior Bordeaux he's drinking with other guests.

Though NPs never buy pictures, they're forever deliberating over whether they might just acquire some eighteenth-century landscape ('to replace the Stubbs we flogged to Paul Mellon'.) With modern pictures they don't even put up a pretence of interest. The price fetched at Christie's for the last auctioned Caravaggio may be indelibly emblazoned on the NP's mind; however, his powers of computation get a bit muddled when trying to assess the value of the work of a recent Slade alumnus or a potential David Hockney.

THE SEASON

Back in the days when the summer months constituted the Season, conforming members of polite society would have been loath to miss any of the exceedingly glamorous events which made up the varied and amusing social calendar. Today, most of the events still take place, but their essential character has changed. Like the once rose damask on the dining-room walls of the NP's parental mansion, their colour has dulled and appeal has faded.

NPs born in today's dismal world feel no pressing compulsion to attend these democratically dreary events that until recently were reserved only for him and his exalted set. What's the fun of nibbling strawberries at Wimbledon while being audially assaulted by loud-mouthed Americans both off court and on it? What joy is there in rubbing shoulder pads with used-car salesmen at first nights at Covent Garden or jostling with spivs and self-publicists at Ascot? Is there still a social preserve for the once upper classes? Few that the NP acknowledges. The last time he watched the flotilla of slender yachts plough through the waters off Cowes was from the stern of his dentist's speedboat.

But two events are still attended by the NP contingent en masse – the Derby ('It was always democratic') and the Fourth of June, Eton's open day for parents (also heavily attended by NP old boys who show up ostensibly to see some cousin or nephew). Here in the sanctity of the Eton grounds plutocracy and pauperdom mix with shameless impunity. Rusted out T-registration Renaults park alongside gleaming Bentleys. Neatly pressed serge ambles past disintegrating twill. Ham sandwiches at one picnic are consumed next to lobster at another. The Fourth of June is England at its most socially privileged and at the same time most financially diverse.

THE DEB SCENE

The deb scene was originally conceived to splice proper young ladies with well-bred men, thus diminishing the chances of unwholesome proletarian cells tainting the azure blue blood of the upper crust. Curiously, the deb scene continues today, having made few concessions to the changing times. Blue blood still meets blue blood – empty wallet pairing off with hollow purse. Where is the transfusion of new money? Rarely to be found in today's deb circus. Peter Townend, the deb impresario, could do well to find some common ground between Debrett's and St John's Wood. Both would be well served.

Still, there are enough drinks parties and dances for the socially committed, sexually unattached NP under twenty-five to have a good and almost free time between the months of May and September, though NPs complain bitterly that the ratio of private dances is losing ground to the ticket-buying charity ones. At £40 for an average double ticket, many NPs fear they are being priced out of the deb market altogether. Some can hardly afford a bun to throw! Others still, who actually have jobs, cannot afford the inevitable hangover.

Yet charm can propel an astute NP through the deb scene on dole money. Desperate mothers of plain daughters will always buy a dance ticket for a socially eligible though financially distressed young man. Curiously, the paradox of being financially distressed *and* eligible never seems to strike hopeful matchmaking mothers.

SPONGING

Where once he was a gracious host, the NP now finds himself unwillingly thrust into the role of grateful guest. No country-house weekend, Riviera villa party or Knightsbridge restaurant is complete without its contingent of NPs shamelessly swilling down Chateau Petrus and scoffing Chateaubriand at their host's expense. Queues of Iranian, American and Continental mega-millionaires seem to feel the NP is a good charitable cause. Today's nouveau riche status symbols are a Rolls in the garage, a Rolex on the wrist and an NP at their table.

Yet the NP would be mortified to be called a sponger and what others call a 'ponce'. No matter how many lobsters, magnums of Bolinger or evenings at Annabels are paid for by patrons, the NP feels his moral slate, at any rate, is clean. The Texan oilionaire, by whose poolside he sips gin and tonic, or on whose ranch he practises polo is merely on the other side of a legitimate social transaction. Petrodollars for pedigree – a pragmatic not parasitic relationship. If he is sponging, then the NP feels it is sponging taken to a higher plane. The ordinary sponger, for want of anything valuable to offer his patron, needs to master the art of toadying and sucking up. But the NP need never demean himself in this unseemly way. It is not for him to make his host feel clever or important. His hosts don't require a court jester at their table; they want a king or count however impecunious. Furthermore, the NP's conversation is likely to be more amusing than a fellow arriviste businessman whose formative years have been spent grappling in the boardroom. At restaurants, however, there is usually one small embarrassing incident for patron and protegé. Owing to the NP's commanding aristocratic demeanour, the waiter invariably places the bill in front of the NP, not his host.

SPONGING ETIQUETTE

If, on invitation, his host has not made it clear that he is going to pick up the tab, the NP should make it discreetly understood that he cannot. This gives the host the option of gracefully withdrawing the invitation. There are no strict social conventions on how this is done and on rare occasions it can be embarrassing – but not as embarrassing as when the NP discovers at the end of the evening, he has been expected to pay his own way all along.

The NP must never offend his host or hostess by sniggering detectably at any display of vulgarity or gaucheness. A transaction of breeding and money requires the NP always to keep his part of the bargain.

DRINKS PARTIES

Unless he's a member of the ultra-young NP set, the NP feels he has fallen too far in the world if he resorts to throwing a Bring a Bottle party. Such social novelties are not for those in the business of keeping up appearances. Well-meaning guests, conscious of the NP's privation, might, however, be so considerate as to bring along a bottle voluntarily. When this happens, offended, yet scrupulously mannered NPs, respond by discreetly depositing the offering in the nearest cupboard while embarrassedly mumbling gratitude.

A bachelor NP, however, might 'share' a drinks party. This does not necessarily mean clubbing together with another NP to divide the onerous task of pouring peanuts into cracked Meissen bowls. Often it means the NP befriending some lonely, socially hopeful foreigner with a superior flat, then acquainting him with all the NP's illustrious friends. In return, the indebted host need merely pick up the £300 tab for drinks and butling services.

When the NP throws a drinks party himself, the quality of the booze and service is usually in inverse proportion to the grandness of his domicile. NPs, embarrassed at living in the socially zero-rated borough of Wandsworth will go to enormous lengths to do everything properly. Domestic agencies are now quite used to sending out troops of butlers and waiters to serve respectable clarets and champagne in the brave new social territories of Stockwell and Clapham, whereas in Chelsea Hirondelle often suffices. This trend has been adopted even by some of the grander ancien riche, much to the disgust of discerning socialites.

Lord Burghersh, the dashing son and heir of the Earl of Westmorland, remarks that the claret now served at parties in the stately drawing-rooms of Belgravia is often barely drinkable. 'It's as if the host is saying he can get away with it because of his smart address,' he declares, adding, 'As a group NPs are easy to identify at other people's drinks parties. They are always the last to leave, and are usually hoping the host and hostess will invite them to stay on for supper.'

Being impecunious themselves never seriously impedes NPs from criticizing the failings of other hosts or hostesses. However, they rarely attack their own kind. What NPs relish is pointing out the social gaffes of the Nouveaux Riches whose parties are their mainstay. Many an impoverished Honourable can be heard rudely complaining at a Nouveau Riche's party about the inferiority of the plonk, the aspic on the smoked salmon sandwiches (sure sign of a downmarket caterer) and the vulgarity of the other guests. One NP at a drinks party boldly strode up to his rich host and advised him to sack his interior decorator because of the gaudiness of his taste. 'My wife decorated the house,' replied the nearly dumb-struck host. 'Grounds for immediate divorce,' countered the unabashed NP, strolling off to refill his glass with Krug.

NP DINNER PARTIES

While serving a delicious soufflé at the end of a spectacular dinner, Cecil Beaton replied in answer to his guests' flattering comments on his lavish hospitality: 'It's just that I'm not grand enough to serve you Mr Kipling's treacle tart.' NPs think they are and often do.

Food and wine at an NP party is the bottom priority. Everything else – i.e. getting out the silver – ranks higher in importance. More and more NPs, however, no longer have any silver. These NPs do not invite their friends to dinner parties; they invite them round for 'supper'. Supper has culinary connotations of 'after the ball' when exhausted and intoxicated dancers attempt to stabilize their stomachs with inexpensive savouries like kedgeree. So giving a supper means not having to lay out the non-existent silver or serving too many courses. 'I warn you,' they breezily declare to their intended guests, 'it won't be anything much.' And usually they're right. It isn't.

Some of the younger NPs have forgotten about starters altogether. Now it is straight on to the main (virtually the only) course followed by cheese and port. Sometimes a bowl of bruised and withered fruit is laid out which is touched by none but the tipsy or famished.

The key word when it comes to dinner-party fare is simplicity. A middle-class suburban housewife might blush with embarrassment serving her guests an indifferent casserole. Not the NPs. They make 'cordon bleu' sound like a nasty foreign habit. 'The royals never eat anything but plain food,' they will aggressively declare as they plonk down some watery stew.

While he is engaging the guests in amusing repartee, the NP husband is content to let his wife traipse from kitchen to table and back again lugging heavy Le Creuset ironware. This often results in misunderstandings with guests from abroad who haven't as yet grasped the full extent of the financial demise of so many of the British upper classes. As one American socialite wrote to her sister who was to visit London for the first time: 'Address the maid who takes your coat as Darling. She is probably your hostess.'

Older NPs, however, still think it important to have someone to help out a dinner party. They never refer to servants as servants any longer (it is too politically loaded) but 'help'. One NP hired 'help' in the form of a headwaiter from a local hotel. Desiring to impress his grand guests he foolishly declared the man was 'a retainer who's been with the family all his life'. But the NP was rumbled when to his horror the rented waiter started serving the surprised guests their vegetables himself, rather than let them help themselves in mandatory country-house style.

However poor they become, there is an ingrained reflex among older NPs to try as hard as they can with dinner parties. The worst that could be said of them is that they heavily economize with their wines. But generally their own standards are so high that quixotically many turn down invitations to grand dinners because they are ashamed they cannot reciprocate.

Among younger NPs dining-room etiquette is often completely abandoned. But this is understandable. Pretence of a smart occasion can be difficult to sustain when eight sit down to dine in their host's bedroom. 'Half of my guests have to perch on my bed,' says the Honourable Rose Cornwallis, who shares a two-roomed basement flat in Fulham. 'Living in one room is all right,' she adds, 'it is the reality of our age.' Many NPs admit to finding these sort of dinner parties more fun than others where an upper-class pretence continues. 'There's a spirit of *fin de siècle*,' explains one NP. 'You become more abandoned and relaxed as you don't have to try and keep up appearances.'

Some, however, don't enjoy their generation's fall from financial grace, especially not in respect to dining out. Biographer Hugo Vickers has one particular trick when he attends what he describes as a typical Fulham dinner party. As it is now mandatory to present a bottle of wine to your host or hostess, and as young NPs cannot afford anything better than plonk, he brings along one extra bottle of a good wine which he discreetly places on the floor next to his chair and proceeds to drink throughout the meal. This is not so much out of meanness, he claims, but because all too often the host takes any bottle of proffered 'good wine' and hides it in the cupboard for his own future use.

As the primary pleasure of a young NP dinner party is the company, not the cuisine, some hosts like to get their guests slightly sloshed before the meal so they won't notice what they're given to eat. If the host is a young man he invariably dishes up a sort of chicken slosh with rice and served with peas. NP women are going more and more for pasta, recognizing perhaps its economic advantages. As a culinary dustbin, pasta is unsurpassable: a few dehydrating mushrooms, a handful of windowsill basil, a clove or two of shrivelled garlic and the cream from yesterday's rhubarb fool can easily be incorporated into an original creation to pour over the fresh green tagliatelle. The unsuspecting guests will be dazzled. Or so goes the NP's rationale.

Despite their nutritionally suspect offerings, NPs of whatever age try extra hard by serving it on good family china, if they've still got it. No matter how small the occasion, the last of these family heirlooms are unobtrusively produced. There may be a chip in the Meissen – decapitating the head of a unicorn – or a crack through a Sèvres rose but the discerning eye will recognize past ancestral glory. For whatever else it lacks, the NP dinner party never fails to provide nostalgic poignancy.

Lady Elizabeth Anson. *PHOTO: LOLO CHILD*

ENTERTAINMENT TIPS FOR NPS

By LADY ELIZABETH ANSON, cousin of the Queen and founder of *Party Planners*

Instead of throwing separate parties for your son's 21st, your daughter's coming out and your own wedding anniversary, why not throw one jolly good party for the whole lot of you. The price of a band is the same price for seventy people as it is for 700.

★

Instead of having your invitations engraved, have them thermographed which is cheaper and gives a raised print. And thermographing on good-quality thick card far outclasses engraving on thinner card.

★

At a wedding serve both good champagne and white plonk for those who don't like bubbles. This way you spend the same that you would have on sparkling wine but you have saved yourself the embarrassment of advertising your reduced circumstances.

★

Put roast beef through the ham slicer. Four paper-thin slices equal one thicker slice with the advantages of taking up more surface area of the plate and therefore convincing your guests that they've been fêted.

★

Make your guests feel exotic, especially at lunchtime by giving them chicken salad with slivers of mango, almonds and other unexpected goodies. You don't need much of the relatively expensive fruit to add a dash of colour and texture, never mind the gorgeous taste.

★

Avoid labour-intensive food. Always calculate the length of preparation as well as the basic cost. For a good summer party meal I recommend a cold cucumber soup and a baby Cornish lobster as you only need to boil it and then cut it in half.

★

If you can't afford smoked salmon, serve the best kedgeree, but don't compromise on the ingredients.

★

You must serve good wines, but Louis Latour tastes just as good with Cottage Pie as it does with Chateaubriand.

★

Trust your own intuition. Don't always do the expected thing. The unusual is always best.

★

NIGHTCLUBS

As a rule, NPs would rather spend an entire evening in a good club like Annabel's and Tramp and drink two glasses of mediocre wine than patronize a lesser club and be given bottles of free vintage champagne. They don't often eat at nightclubs, but when they do it is for one of two reasons: *1)* they are invited to the opening night by the host who mistakenly believes the NP to be well-connected. With such a valuable invitation in hand the NP repays many a favour by bringing along a gaggle of fellow NPs. The result is that the club soon goes bankrupt *2)* a covertly despised foreigner (usually Iranian, Greek or Texan) pays for the privilege of hosting.

NPs keep up their subscription to Annabel's because it is cheap (country membership is £25 p.a. for old members) but they seldom appear in its dazzling inner sanctum before midnight when the club suddenly becomes overcrowded with NPs making one drink last all night. One of Annabel's best-known patrons is St James's art dealer Martin Leggatt. 'I think Annabel's is marvellous,' he said in a recent interview in *Tatler*. 'I only drink Coca-Cola and if the girl has a few cremes de menthe you can get away with an evening's dancing for twelve quid and you're bound to know some people there.'

Raffles is also popular with the NP set but the cheapest place in London is the basement of the Pizza Express on Gloucester Road where NPs congregate after a drinks party. They go in numbers, take it over and manage to bop the night away for about £4 a head including food. The discerning NP drinks soda water in this sort of establishment 'to avoid rot gut, old boy!'

SOCIETIES

Hopelessly destitute NPs have had to give up even their relatively cheap memberships to places like the French and Italian Institutes, the English Speaking Union and the Irish Georgian Society, despite none asking an annual fee exceeding £10. Of all these, the Irish Georgian Society is the most reluctantly abandoned. NP members of this illustrious association run by Desmond Guinness come together to share a common obsession. Assembling at a stately home, members ogle the Titians, Canalettos and Sèvres still safely in the hands of those canny enough to have held on to their fortunes. Afterwards they gather together in order to commiserate over their shared plight and to down vast quantities of anaesthetizing liquid.

THE CLUB

The NP needs his club in nearly the same way he needs oxygen. Upon entering the club's sanctified portals he can breathe again the reassuring, fusty air of decaying gentility, recline in plum leather armchairs and be waited upon by arthritic lackeys while reminiscing of the days when the Empire extended beyond the confines of a cinema in Leicester Square.

No matter how far he might have fallen in the world, the currency of the gentleman's club remains what the NP himself has in surplus – ancestral vintage. In his club the vulgar market-place is forgotten, trade is resurrected as a dirty word and blackballing is a revenge to be taken against parvenu merchants.

No matter that its food is as tasteless as a school dinner. Or that the retainers are deaf and half the members decrepit. So what that he has to cancel his BUPA subscription in order to pay for the club's? The NP's club is his sanctuary; the refuge that denies the unspeakable world outside. Anyway, the NP also knows that his club is much cheaper than hotels and restaurants of equivalent elegance and service where commercial considerations dictate extortionate tariffs. For this reason alone, the older NP remains a member of his club to the point of utter destitution. He might confess to feeling a bit of a cad giving his sister's address in the shires to achieve country status (town membership sometimes costs twice as much). Yet the NP sadly concludes that he can't afford the high price of being a gentleman *all* the time.

LAST RESORTS

We had intended you to be
The next Prime Minister but three
The stocks were sold; the press was
squared;
The middle class was quite prepared.
But as it is! My language fails!
Go out and govern New South Wales!

▪

'Lord Lundy' by HILAIRE BELLOC

Rather than face the igominy and shame of personal bankruptcy, gentlemen are supposed to 'do the decent thing' when they cannot meet sizeable debts, like putting a pistol to their heads or disappearing abroad. However, NPs have pursued other options with varying degrees of success and failure, ranging from the morally distasteful to the outright criminal.

POST-OBITING

Even the most dutiful and affectionate sons have considered post-obiting their beloved father. Post-obiting is raising a loan against the death of a close relation in anticipation of being a major beneficiary in their will. The size of the loan that can be raised depends on the lender's estimate of the relative's life expectancy set against compound interest. The problem here for the NP is that fathers and aged aunts do not take kindly to strangers asking impertinent questions about their soundness in wind and limb. Post-obiting was particularly fashionable in the eighteenth and early nineteenth centuries. The last really famous incident of post-obiting was revealed in 1922, when it transpired the new Duke of Leinster had signed away his lifetime's income of £1.1 million a year (in today's money) in return for an Irish businessman's paying off his debts while he was still heir (see 'Distressed Dukes'). Owing to inflation, punitive taxes on capital and the powers of modern medicine it is said that the rates presently offered in the City for even the most geriatric relative are tempting to only the most desperate of NPs.

KISS'N'SELL

From an early age, aristocrats have been trained to keep their illustrious names out of newspapers other than *The Times* or the *Daily Telegraph*. Until recently some of the Guards regiments even fined officers who, however inadvertently, appeared in a gossip column.

A generation ago, when traditional social mores were still strictly observed, so few aristocrats broke the ban on self-advertisement that when one did, the price he was paid was commensurate with the low supply and high demand of these noble revelations. When Peter Townsend, the much rumoured 'future husband' of Princess Margaret, sold his story to the *Daily Express* he received more than £500,000 in today's money. And in the fifties, the intriguing, yet hardly shameful, newspaper memoirs of the Duke and Duchess of Windsor fetched them £100,000 – in today's money, the exorbitant fee of £800,000.

Nowadays, with more impoverished gentlemen than ever, many a noble lord grants interviews to members of the press in order to entice more visitors to his stately home or to plug a product he is hoping to sell. But most NPs would rather die than shame themselves and their family by confessing unseemly sex-posés, however profitable. In today's torrid tabloid market, it is not enough to regret in public the sad consequences of a failed marriage: for an NP to make 'money' he must not only name adulterous co-respondents, but list their preferred vices and rate their performance. With ageing starlets like baronet's daughter Vicki Hodge copulatin', kissin' 'n' tellin' the confession market has been glutted. The amount of money an NP will receive for his memoirs today is in direct proportion to how many names he can drop and how many

Baronet's daughter Vicki Hodge who broadcast 'love amongst the tropical flowers' for £48,000. *PHOTO: PRESS ASSOCIATION*

Baronet's heir Dai Llewellyn demonstrating his diminishing assets. *PHOTO: ALAN DAVIDSON*

beds he can drop them into.

When Old Etonian, Dai Llewelyn, already heavily featured in the gossip columns, sold his sexploits to the *News of the World* in January 1980 he received the paltry sum of £30,000 (today's money: £42,000). And for this relatively measly financial gain, Dai's social stock plummeted. Dragging out the aristocratic laundry and hanging it on a Fleet Street clothes-line is forgivable in tarts, but not in toffs. Afterwards Dai admitted to being 'ashamed' of what he had done, and yet according to him, 'It was the only measure I could think of at the time to clear off several huge debts.'

The problem for the average NP prepared to tell all, however, is that his sex life would hardly merit a footnote, never mind a series of features.

CRIME AND THE NP

The prototypical upper-class crime for gain was committed by Sir Delves Broughton who, in June 1939, persuaded a broke army officer to make off with some pearls and portraits and then claimed from the insurance company £12,700 (today's money: £190,000).

The problem today is that few NPs have possessions worth anything near that. Presently the most popular criminal avenue open to NPs to clear debts is drug-smuggling which is not to be confused with 'dealing'. 'Smuggling' has connotations of buccaneering bravado; 'dealing', the retail end of the business, smacks of seediness, though it's the dealers who actually employ the NP smuggler. NPs prefer not to smuggle heroin which they do regard ethically as 'dodgy', unlike cocaine and marijuana. 'I'd never smuggle any drug that's addictive!' is the NP's moral retort. Dealers like to employ NPs because of their respectable appearance and will pay young ex-public schoolboys £5,000 a trip plus generous expenses. Other NPs take a more amateur line and invest in ten grams of cocaine in New York or Amsterdam hoping to double their money and clear £250 upon arrival in England.

Apart from the notable exception of an ex-Guards officer who held up a bank, NPs do not tend to go in for armed robbery. As one NP put it: 'It's tempting, but I couldn't bear to saw the barrels off my Purdeys.' When NPs are violent, the motivation is passion, not gain. But among the upper classes even violence has established parameters. On the subject of Lord Lucan's cudgelled nanny, the Earl of Ypres declared: 'I believe anything I have heard or read about it, yet I just can't see Lucan putting a body in a sack!' (sic)

Not being numerate, the NP does not go in for complicated computer-linked scams. He might well invest in a strip joint or massage parlour, but he is not an extortionist and seldom a blackmailer.

Many a young NP fancying himself as a latterday Raffles, has been known 'forgetfully' to pocket the odd silver snuff box, or gold locket at deb dances. This has led to the conspicuously inelegant presence of blue-suited figures from Securicor mingling in among the not so gilded youth at stately-home hoolies.

Other NPs with a criminal bent consider it 'good sport' to make less than grand exits before paying for their claret and steak at West End restaurants. Is it their fault the restaurant was so foolish as to place the fire exit so conveniently near the loos? If that ploy doesn't work out and they are forced to pay the bill, they compensate by pilfering an umbrella or overcoat as they leave. Morally they remain unruffled – even when perpetrating a cheque fraud. It's not so much that they're *stealing*: it's just that others don't need the money as much as they do.

NP girls are not immune to performing criminal acts either. Vanessa Yielding-Little thinks nothing of spending hours cooing into the company phone to her boyfriend in New York. Her friends might even shoplift the odd pair of woolly socks or an 'overpriced hardback' to read on the train on the way home at the weekend.

The nearly perfect NP crime (i.e. clever

and non-violent) was perpetrated in the late seventies. An Old Wykehamist NP placed a number of 'antique' scientific instruments (which he made himself in a garage in Slough) for auction at Sotheby's and Christie's. After reaping exceptional profits for a number of years he was eventually rumbled. To this day he is astonished as to why the judge did not take into account the mitigating circumstances of 'my ingenuity': 'Instead of a more suitable fine, I was sentenced to eighteen months inside,' he splutters indignantly.

The NP criminal who gets caught usually stands trial at Knightsbridge Crown Court or, for more serious crimes, at the Old Bailey. He invariably gets glowing character references from upstanding members of his family or friends. If the NP is lucky he'll get a light jail sentence, frequently suspended. (The Guards officer who held up a bank was given a suspended sentence and sent to a psychiatrist.) However, certain judges relish sentencing 'privileged' ex-public schoolboys to the longest term possible for their crimes.

The NP of the antiques instruments scam was sent to the 'white collar' Ford Open Prison. He was amazed on arrival to meet numerous well-spoken gents who even had their own lunch table. There were former estate agents, solicitors, wine merchants and drug smugglers who had taken to prison life 'like ducks to water', he says. 'Conditions at Open Prison were not dissimilar to public school,' he adds, 'except there was no academic work and the food was better.'

THE FUTURE

FROM PEER TO ETERNITY

'Two generations more I give it. Unless matters change soon we will see, not just the splitting up of large estates into smaller ones, but the total extinction of any sizeable landholdings whatsoever. The day of the big estate – even of the fairly big estate – is nearly over.'

▪

THE DUKE OF DEVONSHIRE

The Duke of Devonshire gives the rich aristocrats only two generations more 'unless matters change soon'. Can they? Can any government really revoke Capital Transfer Tax – the tax that is starting to slice up the big estates. It seems unlikely. The country is committed to a huge programme of public spending for defence and the welfare state: high taxes for the nation; more NPs.

What will eventually happen to the upper classes? Before more of their Constables and Caravaggios are collared by the taxman, scores of squires will surely follow my Lords Brownlow and Brooke to foreign havens for the displaced rich. Those patriotic peers who stay behind will be forever vexed as to whether they actually *do* love their country more than their fast depleting lucre.

Like their departiste predecessors they will have to adapt their noble assumptions and learn for instance the NP definition of a parvenu: somebody whose company you socially disdain but whose company you'd gladly work for. Because gossip columns will continue to bestow their attentions on the titled and their ilk, most NPs will continue to believe that somehow they still are the 'upper' class. And despite their lowly financial state, other people from other sections of society will believe it as well. Even when the House of Lords is eventually abolished the aura of the NP's ancestral legacy will continue to impress – however low the NP eventually falls. Recently Count Zygmunt Zamoyski has been working as a refuse-collector but in the English drawing-rooms of the exiled Polish community, his title and name continue to give him unquestionable social status.

But surely the upper-class ethos, even in its truncated NP form, will disintegrate eventually. It won't be lack of lucre that destroys upper-class tradition but the absence of the environment that breeds it – the public school. Till now, trusts and rich benevolent relatives have been able to bankroll young NPs through this upper-class cultural processing system. But £55,000 to educate each noble sprog privately may well be out of the pockets of dwindling trusts and spinster aunts in years to come. And even parents who could afford it may no longer be so persuaded by the merits of public school when it means they would have to sacrifice annual holidays in the

Carmargue, that cottage in Cornwall, a second car and the redecoration of their four-roomed flat.

So their children will end up going to 'the village school', i.e. the local comprehensive. However much comprehensives change or improve academically in the coming years, they are hardly going to evolve into hotbeds of social elitism. The Honourable Oliver Overdraft who spent his formative years at a 'comp' will not emerge the same as if he had spent five years at Eton. In later years he might assume his parents' values, even their accent, but it is doubtful this will happen if the nation's other little lordlings, ladies and gentlemen are also propelled through the same sociological levelling process.

In an attempt to assimilate into a less rarified Britain, some of the upper classes, both rich and poor, have already jettisoned their cultural identity; some, because they are ashamed of it; others, because they are fearful of the stigma so many attach to it. Some, like Viscount Tony Benn, not only culturally integrate into the society of the common man or try to, but vigorously attack the ethos from which they sprang. However, most NPs prefer to be true to the tribe into which they were born, however anachronistic its tastes, standards and beliefs. They follow one of the precepts of the Communist *Internationale*, believing that there is nothing more despicable than a class traitor.

Carrying the weighty banner of their culture before them, these NPs will struggle on regardless. They know the mighty oak of the upper class is collapsing. They know its trunk is riddled with dry rot and the earth can no longer feed it. But they know its branches still have sap and there will be foliage for a few seasons yet.